Python for Data Science:

A step-by-step Python Programming Guide to Master Big Data, Analysis, Machine Learning, and Artificial Intelligence

Table of Contents

Introduction

Congratulations on purchasing *Python for Data Science: Python Programming Guide to Master Big Data Analysis, Machine Learning, and Artificial Intelligence,* and thank you for doing so.

The following chapters will discuss the core concepts of big data analysis and "Machine Learning" models that are being developed and advanced using Python programming language. This book will provide you overarching guidance on how you can use Python to develop machine learning models using Scikit-Learn and other machine learning libraries. You will start this book by gaining a solid understanding of the basics of machine learning technology and types of machine learning models. It is important to master the concepts of machine learning technology and learn how researchers are breaking the boundaries of data science to mimic human intelligence in machines using various learning algorithms. The power of machine learning technology has already started to manifest in our environment and in our everyday objects. In the first chapter of this book, you will learn the nuances of "12 of the most popular machine learning algorithms", in a very easy to understand language that requires no background in Python coding language and in fact might spike your interest in this field of research. You will learn about the foundational machine learning algorithms namely, supervised, unsupervised, semi-supervised, and reinforcement machine learning algorithms that serve as the skeleton of hundreds of machine learning algorithms being developed every day.

Like most programming languages, Python boasts a number of built-in functions to make your life easier while coding a software program to address a number of business problems. Chapter 2 contains a list of all such built-in functions, methods, and keywords that can be used to easily develop and run advance codes. This chapter will provide details on how Python programming is being used in the development and testing of software programs, machine learning algorithms, and Artificial Intelligence technologies to solve real world problems. These cutting edge technologies have resulted in tools and programs that are being utilized across the industrial spectrum to solve real world problems and become more futuristic.

In the last chapter, you will learn all about big data right from the historical development to the current explosion in this field. The different big data analytic approaches are explained in detail, along with the functioning and applications of big data analytics. This chapter will also dig deep into the data mining process, the benefits of using data mining technology, the challenges facing the data mining technology, and learn about some data mining tools that you can leverage for your business. You will deep dive into the functioning of Scikit-Learn library along with the pre-requisites required to develop a machine learning model using the Scikit-Learn library. A detailed walkthrough with an open source database using illustrations and actual Python code that you can try hands on by following the instructions in this book. There is no better way to learn than to actually get your hands dirty and get real experience of the task. There is also guidance provided on resolving nonlinear issues with "k-nearest neighbor" and "kernel trick algorithms" in this book.

There are plenty of books on this subject on the market, thanks again for choosing this one! Every effort was made to ensure it is full of as much useful information as possible; please enjoy!

CHAPTER 1

Introduction to Machine Learning

The notion of Artificial Intelligence Technology is derived from the idea that computers can be engineered to exhibit human-like intelligence and mimic human reasoning and learning capacities, adapting to fresh inputs and performing duties without needing human intervention. The principle of artificial intelligence encompasses machine learning. Machine Learning Technology (ML) refers to the principle of Artificial Intelligence Technology, which focuses mainly on the designed ability of computers to learn explicitly and self-train, identifying information patterns to enhance the underlying algorithm and making autonomous decisions without human involvement. In 1959, the term "machine learning" was coined during his tenure at IBM by the pioneering gaming and artificial intelligence professor, Arthur Samuel.

Machine learning hypothesizes that contemporary computers can be trained using targeted training data sets, which can readily be tailored to create required functionality. Machine learning is guided by a pattern-recognition method where previous interactions and outcomes are recorded and revisited in a way that corresponds to its present position. Because machines are needed to process infinite volumes of data, with fresh data constantly flowing in, they need to be equipped to adapt to the fresh data without being programmed by a person, considering the iterative aspect of machine learning. Machine learning has close relations with the field of Statistics, which is focused on generating predictions using advanced computing tools and technologies. The research of "mathematical optimization" provides the field of machine learning with techniques, theories, and implementation areas. Machine learning is also referred to as "predictive analytics" in its implementation to address business issues. In ML, the "target" is known as "label," while in statistics, its called "dependent variable." A "variable" in statistics is known as "feature" in ML. And a "feature creation" in ML is known as "transformation" in statistics.

ML technology is also closely related to data mining and optimization. ML and data mining often utilize the same techniques with considerable overlap. ML focuses on generating predictions on the basis of predefined characteristics of the given training data. On the other hand, data mining pertains to the identification of unknown characteristics in a large volume of data. Data mining utilizes many techniques of ML, but with distinct objectives; similarly, machine learning also utilizes techniques of data mining through the "unsupervised learning algorithms" or as a pre-processing phase to enhance the prediction accuracy of the model. The intersection of these two distinct research areas stems from the fundamental assumptions with which they operate. In machine learning, efficiency is generally assessed with regard to the capacity of the model to reproduce known knowledge, while in "knowledge discovery and information mining (KDD)," the main job is to discover new information. An "uninformed or unsupervised" technique, evaluated in terms of known information, will be easily outperformed by other "supervised techniques." On the contrary, "supervised techniques" can not be used in a typical "KDD" task owing to the lack of training data.

Data optimization is another area that machine learning is closely linked with. Various learning issues can be formulated as minimization of certain "loss function" on training data set. "Loss functions" are derived as the difference between the predictions generated by the model being trained and the input data values. The distinction between the two areas stems from the objective of "generalization." Optimization algorithms are designed to decrease the loss of the training data set. The objective of machine learning is to minimize the loss of input data from the real world.

Machine learning has become such a "heated" issue that its definition varies across the world of academia, corporate companies, and the scientific community. Here are some of the commonly accepted definitions from select sources that are extremely known:

- *"Machine learning is based on algorithms that can learn from data without relying on rules-based programming."* – McKinsey.

- *"Machine Learning, at its most basic, is the practice of using algorithms to parse data, learn from it, and then make a determination or prediction about something in the world."* – Nvidia

- "The field of Machine Learning seeks to answer the question, how can we build computer systems that automatically improve with experience, and what are the fundamental laws that govern all learning processes?" – Carnegie Mellon University

- "Machine learning is the science of getting computers to act without being explicitly programmed." – Stanford University

Basic Concepts of Machine Learning

The biggest draw of machine learning is the engineered capability of the system to learn programs from the data automatically instead of manually constructing the program for the machine. Over the last decade, the use of machine learning algorithms expanded from computer science to the industrial world. Machine learning algorithms are capable of generalizing tasks to execute them iteratively. The process of developing specific programs for specific tasks costs a lot of time and money, but occasionally it's just impossible to achieve. On the other hand, ML programming is often feasible and tends to be much more cost effective. The use of machine learning in tackling ambitious issues of widespread importance, such as global warming and depleting underground water levels, is promising with a massive collection of relevant data.

"A break through in machine learning would be worth ten Microsoft."

– Bill Gates

A number of types of machine learning exist today, but the concept of machine learning largely boils down to three components "representation," "evaluation," and "optimization." Here are some of the standard concepts that are applicable to all of them:

Representation

Machine learning models are incapable of directly hearing, seeing, or sensing input examples. Therefore, a data representation is required to supply the model with a useful vantage point into the key qualities of the data. To be able to successfully train a machine learning model selection of key features that best represent the data is very important. "Representation" simply refers to the act of "representing" data points to the computer in a language that it understands using a set of classifiers. A classifier can be defined as "a system that inputs a vector of discrete and or continuous feature values and outputs a single discrete value called class." For a model to learn from the represented data, the training data set or the "hypothesis space" must contain the desired classifier that you want the models to be trained on. Any classifiers that are external to the hypothesis space cannot be learned by the model.

The data features used to represent the input are very critical to the machine learning process. The data features are so important to the development of the desired machine learning model that can easily be the difference between successful and failed machine learning projects. A training data set containing multiple independent "features" that are well correlated with the "class" can make the machine learning much smoother. On the other hand, the class containing complex features may not be easy to learn from for the machine. This often requires the raw data to be processed so that desired features can be constructed from it, to be leveraged for the ML model. The process of deriving features from raw data tends to be the most time consuming and laborious part of the ML project. It is also considered the most creative and interesting part of the project where intuition and trial and error play just as important role as the technical requirements.

The process of ML is not a "one shot process" of developing a training data set and executing it; instead it is an iterative process that requires analysis of the post run output, followed by modification of the training data set and then repeating the whole process all over again. Another reason for the extensive time and effort required to engineer the training data set is domain specificity. Training data set for an e-commerce platform to generate predictions based on consumer behavior analysis will be very different from the training data set required to develop a self driving car. However, the actual machine learning process remains largely the same across industrial domains. No wonder, a lot of research is being done to automate the feature engineering process.

Evaluation

Essentially the process of judging multiple hypotheses or models to choose one model over another is referred to as an evaluation. To be able to differentiate between useful classifiers from the vague ones, an "evaluation function" is required. The evaluation function is also called "objective," "utility," or "scoring" function. The machine learning algorithm has its own internal evaluation function, which tends to be different from the external evaluation function used by the researchers to optimize the classifier. Usually, the evaluation function is defined prior to the selection of the data representation tool as the first step of the project. For example, the machine learning model for a self-driving car has the feature for identification of pedestrians in its vicinity at near zero false negatives and a low false positive as an evaluation function and the pre-existing condition that needs to be "represented" using applicable data features.

Optimization

The process of searching the space of presented models to achieve better evaluations or highest scoring classifier is called "optimization." For algorithms with more than one optimum classifier, the selection of optimization technique is very critical in the determination of the classifier produced and to achieve a more efficient learning model. A variety of off-the-shelf optimizers are available in the market to kick start new machine learning models before eventually replacing them with custom designed optimizers.

Types of Machine Learning

Supervised Machine Learning

"Supervised machine learning" is widely used in predictive big data analysis because they are able to assess and apply the lessons learned from previous iterations and interactions to new data set. These learning algorithms are capable of labeling all their current events based on the instructions provided to efficiently forecast and predict future events. For example, the machine can be programmed to label its data points as "R" (Run), "N" (Negative), or "P" (Positive). The machine learning algorithm then labels the input data as programmed and gets the correct output data. The algorithm compares the production of its own with the "expected or correct" output, identifies potential modifications, and resolves errors to make the model more accurate and smarter. By employing methods like "regression", " prediction", "classification", and "boosting of ingredients" to properly train the learning algorithms, any new input data can be fed to the machine as "target" data set to assemble the learning program as desired. This jump-starts the analysis and propels the learning algorithms to create an "inferred feature," which can be used to generate forecasts and predictions based on output values for future events. Financial organizations and banks, for example, depend heavily on machine-learning algorithms to track credit card fraud and foresee the likelihood of a potential customer not making their loan payments on time.

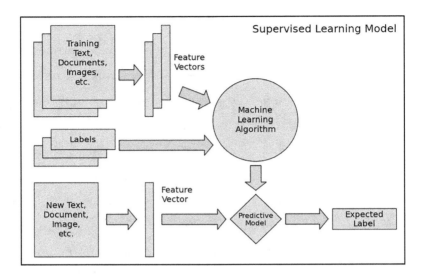

Unsupervised Machine Learning

Companies often find themselves in a situation in which data sources are required to generate a labeled and categorized training data set are unavailable. In these conditions, the use of unsupervised machine learning is ideal. "Unsupervised learning algorithms" are commonly used to describe how the machine can produce "inferred features" to illustrate hidden patterns from an unlabeled and unclassified component in the stack of data. These algorithms can explore the data so that a structure can be defined within the data mass. Although the unsupervised machine learning algorithms are as effective as the supervised learning algorithms in the exploration of input data and drawing insights from it, the unsupervised algorithms are not capable of identifying the correct output. These algorithms can be used to define data outliers; to produce tailor-made product suggestions; to classify text topics using techniques such as "self-organizing maps", "singular value decomposition" and "k-means clustering". Customer identification, for example, customers can be segmented into groups with shared shopping attributes and targeted with similar marketing strategies and campaigns. Consequently, unsupervised learning algorithms are very common in the online marketing industry.

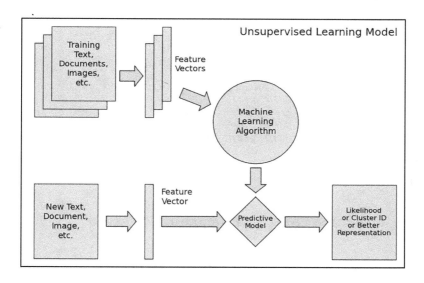

Semi-Supervised Machine Learning

The "semi-supervised machine learning algorithms" are extremely flexible and able to learn from both "labeled" as well as "unlabeled" or raw data. These algorithms are a "hybrid" of supervised and unsupervised ML algorithms. Usually, the training data set consists of predominantly unlabeled data and a tiny portion of labeled data. The use of analytical methods such as the "forecast", "regression" and "classification" in combination with semi-controlled learning algorithms allows the computer to improve its accuracy in learning and training significantly. These algorithms are often used when the production of processed and labeled training data from the raw data set is highly resource-intensive and less cost-effective for the company. Companies are using their systems with semi-supervised learning algorithms to prevent additional personnel and equipment expenses. For example, the application of technology for "facial recognition" requires an enormous quantity of facial data dispersed across multiple input sources. The processing, classification, and labeling of raw data obtained from sources, including internet cameras, require a lot of resources and thousands of hours to be used as a training data set.

Reinforcement Machine Learning

The "reinforcement machine learning algorithm" learns from its environment and is much more unique than any of the previously discussed machine learning algorithms. Such algorithms perform activities and carefully record the results of each action, either as an error for a failed outcome or a reward for excellent results. The two main characteristics that distinguish the reinforcement learning algorithm are the "trial and error" analysis technique and the "delayed reward" feedback loop. The computer continually analyzes input data using a variety of calculations and transmits a signal of reinforcement for each correct or intended output to eventually optimize the final results. The algorithm creates an easy action and rewards feedback loop for assessing, recording, and learning what activity has been efficient, in that it resulted in right or intended output in a shorter time span. The use of such algorithms enables the system to determine optimal conduct automatically and to maximize its effectiveness in a specific context. Therefore, in the disciplines of gaming, robotics, and navigation systems, the reinforcement machine-learning algorithms are heavily utilized.

The machine learning algorithms have proliferated to hundreds and thousands and counting. Here are some of the most widely used algorithms:

1. Regression

The "regression" techniques fall under the category of supervised machine learning. They help predict or describe a particular numerical value based on the set of prior information, such as anticipating the cost of a property based on previous cost information for similar characteristics. Regression techniques vary from simple (such as "linear regression") to complex (such as "regular linear regression", "polynomial regression", "decision trees", "random forest regression" and "neural networks", among others).

The simplest method of all is "linear regression", where the line's "mathematical equation ($y = m*x+b$) is used to model the data collection". Multiple "data pairs (x, y)" can train a "linear regression" model by calculating the position and slope of a line that can decrease the total distance between the data points and the line. In other words, the calculation of the "slope (m)" and "y-intercept (b)" is used for a line that produces the highest approximation for data observations. The data relationships can be modeled with the use of "linear predictor functions", where unidentified model variables can be estimated from the data. These systems are referred to as "linear models". Traditionally, if values of the "explanatory variables" or "predictors" are known, the conditional mean of the response would be used as the "affinity function" of those values. The use of "conditional media" and other measures in linear models is very rare. Similar to every other form of "regression analysis", the "linear regression" also operates on the "conditional probability distribution" of the responses instead of the joint probability distribution of the variables obtained with the multivariate analysis.

The most rigorously researched form of regression analysis with wide applicability has been "linear regression". This emanates from the fact that models that rely linearly on their unidentified parameters are easy to work with compared to the models that are non-linearly related to their parameters. As the statistical characteristics of the resulting predictors can be easily determined with linear distribution.

There are many useful applications of "linear regression", which can be categorized into one of the following:

- If the objective is to generate forecasts and predictions, or to reduce errors, the predictive model can be matched to an identified dataset and explanatory variables with the use of a linear regression algorithm. Once the model has been developed, any new input data without a response can be easily predicted by the fitted model.

- If the objective is to understand variations in the response variables that may be ascribed to variations in the explanatory variables, "linear regression analysis" could be used to quantify the relationship between the predictors and the response specifically, to assess if certain explanatory variables lack any linear relationship with the response. It can also be used to identify subsets of predictors containing any data redundancies pertaining to the response values.

The fitting of most "linear regression models" is accomplished using the "least squares" approach. However, these model can also be fitted by significantly reducing the "lack of fit" in some other standard (just like the "least absolute deviation regression"), or by minimizing a "penalized version of the least square as done in ridge regression (L2-norm penalty) and lasso regression (L1-norm penalty)". By contrast, it is possible to use the "least square" approach to fit machine learning models that are not linear. Therefore, although the terms "least squares" and "linear model" are strongly connected, they are not the same.

"Multiple Linear Regression" tends to be the most common form of "regression" technique used in data science and the majority of statistical tasks. Just like the "linear regression" technique, there will be an output variable "Y" in "multiple linear regression." However, the distinction now is that we're going to have numerous "X" or independent variables generating predictions for "Y".

For instance, a model developed for predicting the cost of housing in Washington DC will be driven by "multiple linear regression" technique. The cost of housing in Washington DC will be the "Y" or dependent variable for the model. "X" or the independent variables for this model will include data points such as vicinity to public transport, schooling district, square footage, and a number of rooms, which will eventually determine the market price of the housing.

The mathematical equation for this model can be written as below:

"housing_price = β_0 + β_1 sq_foot + β_2 dist_transport + β_3 num_rooms"

"Polynomial regression" - Our models developed a straight line in the last two types of "regression" techniques. This straight line is a result of the connection between "X" and "Y" which is "linear" and does not alter the influence "X" has on "Y" as the changing values of "X". Our model will lead in a row with a curve in "polynomial regression".

If we attempted to fit a graph with non-linear features using "linear regression", it would not yield the best fit line for the non-linear features. For instance, the graph on the left shown in the picture below has the scatter plot depicting an upward trend, but with a curve. A straight line does not operate in this situation. Instead, we will generate a line with a curve to match the curve in our data with a polynomial regression, like the chart on the right shown in the picture below. The equation of a polynomial will appear like the linear equation, the distinction being that one or more of the "X" variables will be linked to some polynomial expression. For instance,

$$\text{"Y} = mX^2+b\text{"}$$

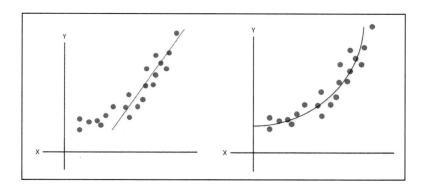

Another significant "regression" technique for data researchers is "Support Vector Regression," which is most frequently used in "case classification." The concept here is to discover a line in space that divides data points into distinct categories. Its also used for regression analysis. It is a form of "binary classification" technique that is not associated with probability.

"Ridge Regression" is a widely used method for analyzing multi-collinear data set. Depending on the features of the data set, using ridge regression correctly can decrease standard errors and significantly improve model accuracy.

Ridge regression can be helpful if your data includes highly correlated independent variables. If you can predict an independent variable with the use of another independent variable, your model will exhibit a high risk of "multi-collinearity." For example, if you use variables that measure the height and weight of a person, these variables in the model are likely to create "multi-collinearity."

Multicollinearity could potentially influence the accuracy of the forecasts and predictions generated by the model. Be mindful of the type of "predictive variables" being utilized in the model to prevent multicollinearity, which could be caused by the type of data you are using, as well as the data collection method. Another reason could be the selection of a small variety of independent variables, or the selection of independent variables was very restricted, which resulted in very similar data points.

Multicollinearity can also be induced by generating a highly specific model. Tor that there are more variables than data points in the model. If you have selected to utilize a "linear model," which ended up worsening the multicollinearity of the model, then you can attempt to implement a method of "ridge regression."

Ridge regression operates to render the predictions more accurate by permitting a hint of bias into the model. This technique is also referred to as "regularization."

Another technique to enhance the accuracy of the model is by "standardizing" the independent variables. The easiest route is to decrease complexity by changing the values of certain independent variables to null. The approach is not simply to modify these independent variables to null but to implement a structure that rewards values closer to zero. This will trigger the coefficients to decrease, so the model's complexity is also reduced, but the model maintains all of its independent variables. This will offer the model more bias, which is a trade-off for increased accuracy of predictions.

Another technique of reduction is called "LASSO regression." A very complementary technique to the "ridge regression," "lasso regression," promotes the use of simpler and leaner models to generate predictions. In lasso regression, the model reduces the value of coefficients relatively more rigidly. LASSO stands for the "least absolute shrinkage and selection operator." Data on our scatterplot, like the mean or median values of the data are reduced to a more compact level. We use this when the model is experiencing high multicollinearity similar to the "ridge regression" model.

A hybrid of "LASSO" and "ridge regression" methods is known as "ElasticNet Regression." Its primary objective is to further enhance the accuracy of the predictions generated by the "LASSO regression" technique. "ElasticNet Regression" is a confluence of both "LASSO" and "ridge regression" techniques of rewarding smaller coefficient values. All three of these designs are available in the R and Python "Glmnet suite."

"Bayesian regression" models are useful when there is a lack of sufficient data, or the available data has poor distribution.

These regression models are developed based on probability distributions rather than data points, meaning the resulting chart will appear as a bell curve depicting the variance with the most frequently occurring values in the center of the curve. The dependent variable "Y" in "Bayesian regression" is not valuation but a probability. Instead of predicting a value, we try to estimate the probability of an occurrence. This is regarded as "frequentist statistics," and this sort of statistic is built on the "Bayes theorem." "Frequentist statistics" hypothesize if an event is going to occur and the probability of it occurring again in the future.

"Conditional probability" is integral to the concept of "frequentist statistics." Conditional probability pertains to the events whose results are dependent on one another. Events can also be conditional, which means the preceding event can potentially alter the probability of the next event. Assume you have a box of M&Ms , and you want to understand the probability of withdrawing distinct colors of the M&Ms from the bag. If you have a set of 3 yellow M&Ms and 3 blue M&Ms, and on your first draw, you get a blue M&M, then with your next draw from the box, the probability of taking out a blue M&M will be lower than the first draw. This is a classic example of "conditional probability." On the other hand, an independent event is flipping of a coin, meaning the preceding coin flip doesn't alter the probability of the next flip of the coin. Therefore, a coin flip is not an example of "conditional probability."

2. Classification

The "classification algorithm" in machine learning and statistics can be defined as the algorithm used to define the set of categories (sub-populations) that the new input data can be grouped under, based on the training dataset, which is composed of related data whose category has already been identified. For instance, all incoming emails can be grouped under the "spam" or "non-spam" category based on predefined rules. Similarly, a patient diagnosis can be categorized on the basis of the patient's observed attributes such as gender, blood group, prominent symptoms, family history for genetic diseases. Classification" can be considered as a type of pattern recognition technology. These individual hypotheses can be analyzed into a set of properties that can be easily quantified, referred to as "explanatory variables or features." These can be classified as "categorical", for example, different types of blood groups like 'A+', 'O-'; or "ordinal" for example, different types of sizes like large, small; or "integer values," for example, number of times a specific word is repeated in a text; or "real values," for example, height and weight measurement. Certain classifiers operate by drawing a comparison with their prior observations using a "similarity or distance function."

Any machine learning algorithm that is capable of implementing classification, particularly in the context of model implementation, is called "classifier." Very often, the term "classifier" is used in the context of the mathematical function, which is being implemented by a "classification algorithm" and can map new input to the appropriate category. In the field of statistics, the classification of data is often carried out with "logistic regression," wherein the characteristics of the observations are referred to as "explanatory variables" or "independent variables" or "regressors" and the categories used to generate predictions are known as "outcomes." These "outcomes" are regarded as the probable values of the dependent variable. In the context of machine learning, "observations are often referred to as instances, the explanatory variables are referred to as features (grouped into a feature vector) and the possible categories to be predicted are referred to as classes."

The "Logistic regression" technique is "borrowed" by ML technology from the world of statistical analysis. "Logistic regression" is regarded to be the simplest algorithm for classification, even though the term sounds like a technique of "regression," that is not the case. "Logistic regression" produces estimates on the basis of single or multiple input values for the likelihood of an event occurring. For example, a "logistic regression" will use a patient's symptoms, blood glucose level , and family history as inputs to generate the likelihood of the patient to develop diabetes. The model will generate a prediction in the form of probability ranging from '1' to '10' where '10' means full certainty. For the patient, if the projected probability exceeds 5, the prediction would be that they will suffer from diabetes. If the predicted probability is less than 5, it would be predicted that the patient will not develop diabetes. Logistic regression allows a line graph to be created, which can represent the "decision boundary."

It is widely used for binary classification tasks that involve two different class values. Logistic regression is so named owing to the fundamental statistical function at the root of this technique called the "logistic function." Statisticians created the "logistic function," also called the "sigmoid function," to define the attributes of population growth in ecosystems, which continues to grow rapidly and nearing the maximum carrying capacity of the environment. The logistic function is "an S-shaped curve capable of taking any real-valued integer and mapping it to a value between '0' and '1', but never precisely at those boundaries, where 'e' is the base of the natural log (Euler's number or the EXP)" and the numerical value that you are actually going to transform is called the 'value.'

"1 / (1 + e^-value)"

Here is a graph of figures ranging from "-5 and 5" which has been transformed by the logistic function into a range between 0 and 1.

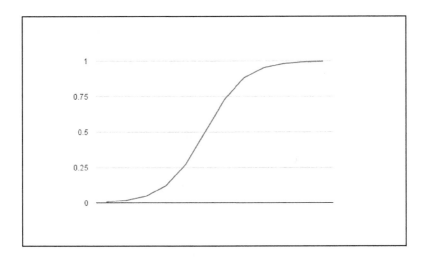

Similar to the "linear regression" technique, "logistic regression" utilizes an equation for data representation.

Input values (X) are grouped linearly to forecast an output value (Y), with the use of weights or coefficient values (presented as the symbol "Beta"). It is mainly different from the "linear regression" because the modeled output value tends to be binary (0 or 1) instead of a range of values.

Below is an example of the "logistic regression" equation, where "the single input value coefficient (X) is represented by 'b1', the "intercept or bias term' is the 'bo', and the "expected result" is 'Y'. Every column in the input data set has a connected coefficient "b" with it, which should be understood by learning the training data set. The actual model representation, which is stored in a file or in the system memory, would be "the coefficients in the equation (the beta values)."

$$y = e^{\wedge}(b0 + b1*x)/(1 + e^{\wedge}(b0 + b1*x))$$

The "logistic regression" algorithm's coefficients (the beta values) must be estimated on the basis of the training data. This can be accomplished using another statistical technique called "maximum-likelihood estimation," which is a popular ML algorithm utilized using a multitude of other ML algorithms. "Maximum-likelihood estimation" works by making certain assumptions about the distribution of the input data set.

An ML model that can predict a value nearer to "0" for the "other class" and a value nearer to "1" for the "default class" can be obtained by employing the best coefficients of the model. The underlying assumption for most likelihood of the "logistic regression" technique is that "a search procedure attempts to find values for the coefficients that will reduce the error in the probabilities estimated by the model pertaining to the input data set (e.g., probability of '0' if the input data is not the default class)".

Without going into mathematical details, it is sufficient to state that you will be using "a minimization algorithm to optimize the values of the best coefficients from your training data set." In practice, this can be achieved with the use of an effective "numerical optimization algorithm," for example, the "Quasi-newton" technique).

3. Clustering

We enter the category of unsupervised machine learning, with "clustering methods" because its objective is to "group or cluster observations with comparable features". Clustering methods do not use output data to train but allow the output to be defined by the algorithm. Only data visualizations can be used in clustering techniques to check the solution's quality.

"K-Means clustering", where 'K' is used to represent the number of "clusters" that the customer elects to generate and is the most common clustering method. (Note that different methods for selecting K value, such as the "elbow technique," are available.)

Steps used by K-Means clustering to process the data points:

1. The data centers are selected randomly by 'K'.

2. Assigns each data point to the nearest centers that have been randomly generated.

3. Re-calculates each cluster's center.

4. If centers do not change (or have minor change), the process will be completed.

Otherwise, we'll go back to step 2. (Set a maximum amount of iterations in advance to avoid getting stuck in an infinite loop, if the center of the cluster continues to alter.)

The following plot applies "K-Means" to a building data set. Each column in the plot shows each building's efficiency. The four measurements relate to air conditioning, heating, installed electronic appliances (refrigerators, TV), and cooking gas. For simplicity of interpretation of the results, 'K' can be set to value '2' for clustering, wherein one cluster will be selected as an efficient building group and the other cluster as an inefficient building group. You see the place of the structures on the left as well as a couple of the building characteristics used as inputs on the right: installed electronic appliances and heating.

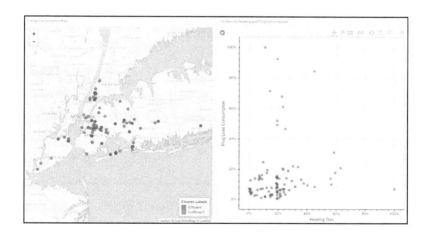

4. Dimension Reduction

As the name indicates, to extract the least significant information (sometimes redundant columns) from a data set, we use "dimensionality reduction." In practice, data sets tend to contain hundreds or even thousands of rows (also known as characteristics), which makes it essential to reduce the total number of rows. For example, pictures may contain thousands of pixels; all those pixels are not important for the analysis. Or a large number of measurements or experiments can be applied to every single chip while testing microchips within the manufacturing process, the majority of which produce redundant data. In such scenarios, "dimensionality reduction" algorithms are leveraged to manage the data set.

Principal Component Analysis

"Principal Component Analysis" or (PCA) is the most common "dimension reduction technique," which decreases the size of the "feature space" by discovering new vectors that are capable of maximizing the linear variety of the data. When the linear correlations of the data are powerful, PCA can dramatically decrease the data dimension without losing too much information. PCA is one of the fundamental algorithms of machine learning. It enables you to decrease the data dimension, losing as little information as possible.

It is used in many fields such as object recognition, vision of computers, compression of information, etc. The calculation of the main parts is limited to the calculation of the initial data's own vectors and covariance matrix values or to the data matrix's unique decomposition. Through one we can convey several indications, merge, so to speak, and operate with a simpler model already. Of course, most probably, data loss will not be avoided, but the PCA technique will assist us to minimize any losses.

t-Stochastic Neighbor Embedding (t-SNE)

Another common technique is "t-Stochastic Neighbor Embedding (t-SNE)," which results in a decrease of non-linear dimensionality. This technique is primarily used for data visualization, with potential use for machine learning functions such as space reduction and clustering.

The next plot demonstrates the "MNIST database" analysis of handwritten digits. "MNIST" includes a large number of digit pictures from 0 to 9, used by scientists to test "clustering" and "classification" algorithms. The individual row of the data set represents the "vectorized version" of the original picture (size 28x28 = 784 pixels) and a label (0, 1, 2, and so on) for each picture. Note that the dimensionality is therefore reduced from 784 pixels to 2-D in the plot below. Two-dimensional projecting enables visualization of the initial high-dimensional data set.

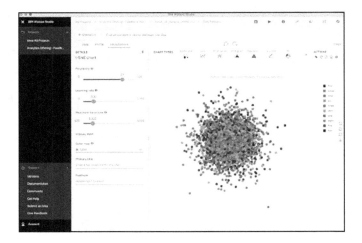

5. Ensemble Methods

Think that you have chosen to construct a car because you are not pleased with the variety of cars available in the market and online. You may start by discovering the best option for every component that you need. The resulting car will outshine all the other alternatives with the assembly of all these excellent components.

"Ensemble methods" use the same concept of mixing several predictive models (controlled machine learning) to obtain results of greater quality than any of the models can generate on their own. The "Random Forest" algorithms, for instance, is an "ensemble method" that collates various trained "Decision Trees" with different data set samples. Consequently, the quality of predictions generated by "Random Forest" method is better than the quality of the estimated predictions generated by only one "Decision Tree."

Think of "ensemble methods" as an approach for reducing a single machine learning model's variance and bias. This is essential because, under certain circumstances, any specified model may be accurate but completely incorrect under other circumstances. The relative accuracy could be overturned with another model. The quality of the predictions is balanced by merging the two models.

6. Transfer Learning

Imagine you are a data scientist focusing on the clothing industry. You have been training a high-quality learning model for months to be able to classify pictures of "women's tops" as tops, tank tops, and blouses. You have been tasked to create a comparable model for classification of pants pictures such as jeans, trousers, and chinos. With the use of "Transfer Learning" method, the understanding incorporated into the first model be seamlessly transferred and applied to the second model.

Transfer Learning pertains to the re-use and adaptation of a portion of a previously trained neural network to a fresh but comparable assignment. Specifically, once a neural network has been successfully trained for a particular task, a proportion of the trained layers can be easily transferred and combined with new layers that are then trained on pertinent data for the new task. This new "neural network" can learn and adapt rapidly to the new assignment by incorporating a few layers.

The primary benefit of transferring learning is decrease in the volume of data required to train the neural network resulting in cost savings for the development of "deep learning algorithms." Not to forget how hard it can be to even procure a sufficient amount of labeled data to train the model.

Suppose in this example/ ; you are using a neural network with 20 hidden layers for the "women's top" model. You understand after running a few tests that 16 of the women's top model layers can be transferred and combined them with a new set of data to train on pants pictures. Therefore, the new pants model will have 17 concealed layers. The input and output of both the tasks are distinct, but the reusable layers are capable of summarizing the data appropriate to both, e.g., clothing, zippers, and shape of the garment.

Transfer learning is getting increasingly popular, so much so that for basic "deep learning tasks" such as picture and text classification, a variety of high quality pre-trained models are already available in the market.

7. Natural Language Processing

A majority of the knowledge and information pertaining to our world is in some type of human language. Once deemed as impossible to achieve, today, computers are capable of reading large volumes of books and blogs within minutes. Although computers are still unable to fully comprehend "human text," but they can be trained to perform specific tasks. Mobile devices, for instance, can be trained to auto-complete text messages or fix spelling mistakes. Machines have been trained enough to hold straightforward conversations like humans.

"Natural Language Processing" (NLP) is not exactly a method of ML; instead, it is a commonly used technique to produce texts for machine learning. Consider a multitude of formats of tons of text files (words, internet blogs, etc.). Most of these text files are usually flooded with typing errors, grammatically incorrect characters and phrases that need to be filtered out. The most popular text processing model available in the market today is "NLTK (Natural Language ToolKit)," developed by "Stanford University" researchers.

The easiest approach to map texts into numerical representations is calculation of the frequency of each word contained in every text document. For example, an integer matrix where individual rows represent one text document and every column represents a single word. This word frequency representation matrix is frequently referred to as the "Term Frequency Matrix" (TFM). From there, individual matrix entries can be separated by weight of how essential every single term is within the whole stack of papers. This form of the matrix representation of a text document is called "Term Frequency Inverse Document Frequency" (TFIDF), which usually yields better performance for machine learning tasks.

8. Word Embedding

"Term Frequency Matrix" and "Term Frequency Inverse Document Frequency" are numerical representations of text papers that only take into account frequency and weighted frequencies to represent text files. On the other hand, "Word Embedding" in a document is capable of capturing the actual context of a word. Embedding can quantify the similarity between phrases within the context of the word, which subsequently allows the execution of arithmetic operations with words.

"Word2Vec" is a neural network based technique that can map phrases to a numerical vector in a corpus. These vectors are then used to discover synonyms, do arithmetic with words or phrases, or to represent text files. Let's suppose, for instance, a large enough body of text files was used to estimate word embedding. Suppose the words "king, queen, man, and female" are found in the corpus, and vector ("word") is the number vector representing the word "word". We can conduct an arithmetic procedure with numbers to estimate vector('woman'):

vector('king') + vector('woman') — vector('man') ~ vector('queen')

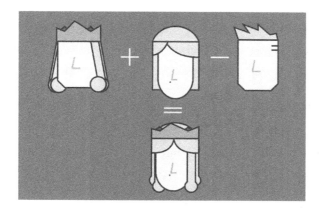

Word depictions enable similarities to be found between phrases by calculating the "cosine similarity" between the vector representation of the two words. The "cosine similarity" gives a measure of the angle between two vectors.

We use machine learning techniques to calculate word embedding, but this is often a preliminary step in implementing a machine learning algorithm on top of the word embedding method. For example, the "Twitter" user database containing a large volume of "tweets" can be leveraged to understand which of these customers purchased a house recently. We can merge "Word2Vec" with logistic regression to generate predictions on the likelihood of a new "Twitter" user purchasing a home.

9. Decision Trees

To refresh your memory, a machine learning decision tree can be defined as "a tree like graphical representation of the decision making process, by taking into consideration all the conditions or factors that can influence the decision and the consequences of those decisions." Decision trees are considered one of the simplest "supervised machine learning algorithms," with three main elements: "branch nodes" representing conditions of the data set, "edges" representing the ongoing decision process and "leaf nodes" representing the end of the decision.

The two types of decision trees are: "Classification tree" that is used to classify Data on the basis of the existing data available in the system; "Regression tree" which is used to make a forecast for predictions for future events on the basis of the existing data in the system. Both of these trees are heavily used in machine learning algorithms. A widely used terminology for decision trees is "Classification and Regression trees" or "CART".

Let's look at how you can build a simple decision tree based on a real-life example.

Step 1: Identify what decision needs to be made, which will serve as a "root node" for the decision tree. For this example, a decision needs to be made on "What would you like to do over the weekend?". Unlike real trees, the decision tree has its roots on top instead of the bottom.

Step 2: Identify conditions or influencing factors for your decision, which will serve as "branch nodes" for the decision tree. For this example, conditions could include "would you like to spend the weekend alone or with your friends?" and "how is the weather going to be?".

Step 3: As you answer the conditional questions, you may run into additional conditions that you might have ignored. You will now continue to your final decision by processing all the conditional questions individually; these bifurcations will serve as "edges" of your decision tree.

Step 4: Once you have processed all of the permutations and combinations and eventually made your final decision, that final decision will serve as the "leaf node" of your decision tree. Unlike "branch nodes," there are no further bifurcations possible from a "leaf node."

Here is the graphical representation of your decision for the example above:

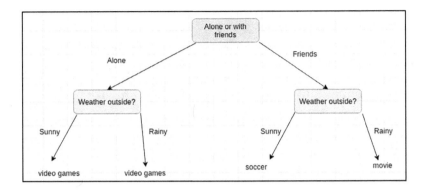

As you would expect from a decision tree, you have obtained a "model representing a set of sequential and hierarchical decisions that ultimately lead to some final decision." This example is at a very high-level to help you develop an understanding of the concept of decision trees. The data science and machine learning decision trees are much more complicated and bigger with hundreds and thousands of branch nodes and edges.

The best tool on the market to visualize and understand decision trees is "Scikit Learn." Machine learning decisions tree models can be developed using two steps: "Induction" and "Pruning."

Induction

In this step, the decision trees are actually developed by selecting and modeling all of the sequential and hierarchical decision boundaries on the basis of the existing data set. For your ease of understanding, here are 4 high level steps required to develop the tree:

1. Gather, classify, and label the training data set with "feature variables" and "classification or regression output."

2. Identify the best and most cost effective feature within the training data set that will be used as the point for bifurcating the data.

3. Based on the possible values of the selected "best feature," create subsets of data by bifurcating the data set. These bifurcations will define the "branch nodes" of the decision tree, wherein each node serves as a point of bifurcation based on specific features from the data set.

4. Iteratively develop new tree nodes with the use of data subsets gathered from step 3. These bifurcations will continue until an optimal point is reached, where maximum accuracy is achieved while minimizing the number of bifurcations or nodes.

Pruning

The inherent purpose of decision trees is to support training and self learning of the system, which often requires over loading of all possible conditions and influencing factors that might affect the final result. To overcome the challenge of setting the correct output for the least number of instances per node, developers make a "safe bet" by settling for that "least number" as rather small. This results in a high number of bifurcations on necessary, making for a very complex and large decision tree. This is where "tree pruning" comes into the picture. The verb "prune" literally means "to reduce especially by eliminating superfluous matter". This is the same kind of concept taken from real life tree pruning and applied to the data science and machine learning decision tree pruning process.

The process of pruning effectively reduces the overall complexity of the decision tree by "transforming and compressing strict and rigid decision boundaries into generalized and smooth boundaries." The number of bifurcations in the decision trees determines the overall complexity of the tree. The easiest and widely used pruning method is reviewing individual branch nodes and evaluating the effect of its removal on the cost function of the decision tree. If the cost function has little to no effect of the removal, then the branch node under review can be easily removed or "pruned."

10. Apriori machine learning algorithm

"Apriori algorithm" is another unsupervised ML algorithm that can produce rules of the association from a specified set of data. "Association rule" simply means if an item X exists, then the item Y has a predefined probability of existence. Most rules of association are produced in the format of "IF-THEN" statements. For instance, "IF" someone purchases an iPhone, "THEN" they have most likely purchased an iPhone case as well. The Apriori algorithm is able to draw these findings by initially observing the number of individuals who purchased an iPhone case while making an iPhone purchase and generating a ratio obtained by dividing the number individuals who bought a new iPhone (1000) with individuals who also bought an iPhone case (800) with their new iPhones.

The fundamental principles of Apriori ML Algorithm are:

- If a set of events have high frequency of occurrence, then all subsets of that event set will also have high frequency of occurrence.

- If a set of events occur occasionally, then all supersets of the event set of will occur occasionally as well.

Apriori algorithm has wide applicability in the following areas:

"Detecting Adverse Drug Reactions"

"Apriori algorithm" is used to analyze healthcare data such as the drugs administered to the patient, characteristics of each patient, harmful side effects experienced by the patient, the original diagnosis, among others. This analysis generates rules of association that provide insight into the characteristic of the patient and the administered drug that potentially contributed to adverse side effects of the drug.

"Market Basket Analysis"

Some of the leading online e-commerce businesses, including "Amazon," use Apriori algorithm to gather insights on products that have high likelihood of being bought together and products that can have an upsell with product promotions and discount offers. For instance, Apriori could be used by a retailer to generate predictions such as: customers purchasing sugar and flour have a high likelihood of purchasing eggs to bake cookies and cakes.

"Auto-Complete Applications"

The highly cherished auto-complete feature on "Google" is another common Apriori application. When the user starts typing in their keywords for a search, the search engine searches its database for other related phrases that are usually typed in after a particular word.

11. Support vector machine learning algorithm

"Support Vector Machine" or (SVM) is a type of "supervised ML algorithm," used for "classification" or "regression," where the data set trains SVM on "classes" in order to be able to classify new inputs. This algorithm operates by classifying the data into various "classes" by discovering a line (hyper-plane) that divides the collection of training data into "classes." Due to the availability of various linear hyper-planes, this algorithm attempts to maximize the distance between the different "classes" involved, which is called "margin maximization." By identifying the line that maximizes the class distance, the likelihood of generalizing apparent to unseen data can be improved.

SVM's can be categorized into two as follows:

- "Linear SVM's" – The training data or classifiers can be divided by a hyper-plane.

- "Non-Linear SVM's" – Unlike linear SVMs, in "non-linear SVM's" the possibility to separate the training data with a hyper-plane is nonexistent. For example, the Face Detection training data consists of a group of facial images and another group of non-facial images. The training data is so complicated under such circumstances that it is difficult to obtain a feature representation of every single vector. It is extremely complex to separate the facial data set linearly from the non-facial data set.

SVM is widely used by different economic organizations for stock market forecasting. For example, SVM is leveraged to compare relative stock performances of various stocks in the same industrial sector. The classifications generated by SVM, aids in the investment related decision-making process.

The Kernel Trick

The data collected in the real world is randomly distributed and making it too difficult to separate different classes linearly. However, if we can potentially figure out a way to map the data from 2-dimensional space to 3-dimensional space, as shown in the picture below, we will be able to discover a decision surface that obviously separates distinct classes.

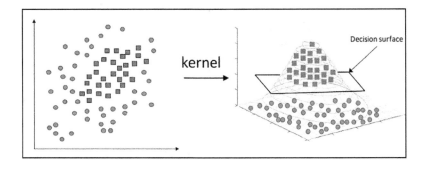

One approach to transform data like this is mapping all data points to a higher dimension (in this case, 3 dimensions), finding the limit, and making the classification. That works for a limited number of dimensions, but computations within a given space become increasingly costly when there are a lot of dimensions to deal with. And so the kernel trick comes to the rescue!

The "kernel trick" enables us to function in the original feature space without needing to calculate the data coordinates in a higher dimensional space. For example, the equation in the picture below has a couple of 3-D data points as 'x' and 'y.'

$$\mathbf{x} = (x_1, x_2, x_3)^T$$
$$\mathbf{y} = (y_1, y_2, y_3)^T$$

Suppose we want to map 'x' and 'y' to 9-dimensional space. To get the final outcome, which would be just scalar, we have to do the calculations shown in the picture below. In this case, the computational complexity will be O(n2).

$$\phi(\mathbf{x}) = (x_1^2, x_1 x_2, x_1 x_3, x_2 x_1, x_2^2, x_2 x_3, x_3 x_1, x_3 x_2, x_3^2)^T$$
$$\phi(\mathbf{y}) = (y_1^2, y_1 y_2, y_1 y_3, y_2 y_1, y_2^2, y_2 y_3, y_3 y_1, y_3 y_2, y_3^2)^T$$

$$\phi(\mathbf{x})^T \phi(\mathbf{y}) = \sum_{i,j=1}^{3} x_i x_j y_i y_j$$

However, by using the "kernel function," which is denoted as 'k (x, y)', instead of doing the complex calculations in the 9-dimensional space, the same outcome can be achieved in the 3-dimensional space by calculating the "dot product" of 'x-transpose' and 'y'. In this case, the computational complexity will be O(n).

$$k(\mathbf{x}, \mathbf{y}) = (\mathbf{x}^T \mathbf{y})^2$$
$$= (x_1 y_1 + x_2 y_2 + x_3 y_3)^2$$
$$= \sum_{i,j=1}^{3} x_i x_j y_i y_j$$

In principle, the kernel trick is used to make the transformation of data into higher dimensions much more effective and less costly. The use of the kernel trick is not restricted to the SVM algorithm. The kernel trick can be used with any computations involving the "dot products (x, y)".

Importance of Machine Learning

The seemingly unstoppable interest in ML stems from the same variables that have made "data mining" and "Bayesian analysis" more common than ever before. The underlying factors contributing to this popularity are increasing quantities and data varieties, cheaper and more effective computational processing, and inexpensive data storage. To get a sense of how significant machine learning is in our everyday lives, it is simpler to state what part of our cutting edge way of life has not been touched by it. Each aspect of human life is being impacted by the "smart machines" intended to expand human capacities and improve efficiencies. Artificial Intelligence and machine learning technology is the focal precept of the "Fourth Industrial Revolution" that could possibly question our thoughts regarding being "human".

All of these factors imply that models that can analyze larger, more complicated data while delivering highly accurate results in a short period of time can be produced rapidly and automatically on a much larger scale. Companies can easily identify potential growth opportunities or avoid unknown hazards by constructing desired machine learning models that meet their business requirements. Data runs through the vein of every company. Increasingly, data-driven strategies create a distinction between winning or losing the competition. Machine learning offers the magic of unlocking the importance of business and customer data to lead to actionable measures and decisions that can skyrocket a company's business and market share.

Machine learning has demonstrated over the recent years that many distinct tasks can be automated, which were once deemed as activities only people could carry out, such as image recognition, text processing, and gaming. In 2014, Machine Learning and AI professionals believed the board game "Go" would take at least ten years for the machine to defeat its greatest player in the world. But they were proved mistaken by "Google's DeepMind", which showed that machines are capable of learning which moves to take into account even in such a complicated game as "Go". In the world of gaming, machines have seen many more innovations such as "Dota Bot" from the "OpenAI" team. Machine learning is bound to have enormous economic and social impacts on our day to day lives. Complete set of work activities and the entire industrial spectrum could potentially be automated, and the labor market will be transformed forever.

"Machine learning is a method of data analysis that automates analytical model building. It is a branch of artificial intelligence based on the idea that systems can learn from data, identify patterns, and make decisions with minimal human intervention."

- SAS

Repetitive Learning Automation and Information Revelation

Unlike robotic automation driven by hardware that merely automates manual tasks, machine learning continuously and reliably enables the execution of high quantity, high volume, and computer-oriented tasks. Artificial intelligence machine learning algorithms help to adapt to the changing landscape by enabling a machine or system to learn, to take note of, and to reduce its previous mistakes. Machine learning algorithm works as a classifier or a forecasting tool to develop unique abilities and to define data patterns and structure. For instance, an algorithm for machine learning has created a model that will teach itself how to play chess and even how to create product suggestions based on consumer activity and behavioral data. This model is so effective because it can easily adjust to any new data set.

Machine learning allows the assessment of deeper and wider data sets by means of neural networks comprising several hidden layers. Just a couple of years ago, a scheme for detecting fraud with countless hidden layers would have been considered a work of imagination. A whole new world is on the horizon with the emergence of big data and unimaginable computer capabilities. The data on the machines is like the gas on the vehicle; more data addition leads to faster and more accurate results. Deep learning models thrive with a wealth of data because they benefit from the information immediately. The machine-learning algorithms have led to incredible accuracy through the «deep neural networks». Increased accuracy is obtained from deep learning, for instance, from the regular and extensive use of smart technology such as "Amazon Alexa" and "Google Search." These "deep neural networks" also boost our healthcare sector. Technologies like image classification and the recognition of objects are now able to detect cancer with the same precision as a heavily qualified radiologist on MRIs.

Artificial intelligence enables the use of big data analytics in combination with the algorithm for machine learning to be enhanced and improved. Data has developed like its own currency and can readily become "intellectual property" when algorithms are self-learning. The crude information is comparable to a gold mine in that the more and more you dig, the more you can dig out or extract "gold" or meaningful insights. The use of machine learning algorithms for the data allows the faster discovery of the appropriate solutions and can make these solutions more useful. Bear in mind that the finest data will always be the winner, even though everyone uses similar techniques.

"Humans can typically create one or two good models a week; machine learning can create thousands of models a week."

- Thomas Davenport, The Wall Street Journal

CHAPTER 2

Python Coding Functions and Applications

Regarded as an extremely user-friendly and simple to learn programming language for entry level programmers and amateurs, Python was first implemented in 1989. It is a high-level programming language, commonly used for general purposes. It was originally developed by Guido van Rossum at the "Center Wickenden & Informatica (CWI), Netherlands," in the 1980s and introduced by the "Python Software Foundation" in 1991. It was designed primarily to emphasize readability of programming code, and its syntax enables programmers to convey ideas using fewer lines of code. Python programming language increases the speed of operation while allowing for higher efficiency in creating system integrations. It is regarded ideal for individuals newly interested in programming or coding and needs to comprehend programming fundamentals. This stems from the fact that Python reads almost the same as the English language. Therefore, it requires less time to understand how the language works and focus can be directed in learning the basics of programming.

Python is an interpreted language that supports automatic memory management and object-oriented programming. This extremely intuitive and flexible programming language can be used for coding projects such as: machine learning algorithms, web applications, data mining and visualization, game development.

Python Built-in Functions

Like most programming languages, Python boasts a number of built-in functions to make your life easier while coding a software program. Here is a list of all such built-in functions:

Function	Description
abs ()	Will result in the absolute values of the numbers.
all ()	Will result in True if all items within an iterative object are true.
any ()	Will result in True if any item of the iterative object holds true.

ascii ()	Will result in a readable version of an object and replace non-ascii characters with escape characters.
bin ()	Will result in the binary version of the numbers.
bool ()	Will result in the boolean values of indicated objects.
bytearray ()	Will result in an array of bytes.
bytes ()	Will result in bytes objects.
callable ()	Will result in True if a specific object is callable or else results in False.
chr ()	Will result in a character from the indicated Unicode code.
classmethod ()	Will convert any method into class method.
compile ()	Will result in the indicated source as an object, ready for execution.
complex ()	Will result in a complex number.
delattr ()	Will delete specific attributes (property or method) from the indicated object.
dict ()	Will result in a dictionary.
dir ()	Will result in a list of properties and methods of the specific object.
divmod ()	Will result in the quotient and the remainder when one argument is divided by another.

enumerate ()	Will take a collection and result in enumerate objects.
eval ()	Will evaluate and execute an expression.
exec ()	Will execute the indicated code (or object)
filter ()	Uses a filter function to exclude items in an iterative object.
float ()	Will result in floating point numbers.
format ()	Will format the indicated value.
frozenset ()	Will result in a frozen set object.
getattr ()	Will result in the value of the indicated attribute (property or method).
globals ()	Will result in the most recent global symbol table as a dictionary.
hasattr ()	Will result in True if the indicated object has the indicated attribute.
hash ()	Will result in the hash value of the indicated object.
help ()	Will execute the built-in help system.
hex ()	Conversion of numbers into hexadecimal values.
id ()	Will result in the identity of an object.
input ()	Will allow user input.
int ()	Will result in an integer number.

isinstance ()	Will result in True if the indicated object is an instance of the indicated object.
issubclass ()	Will result in True if the indicated class is a subclass of the indicated object.
iter ()	Will result in an iterative object.
len ()	Will result in the length of an object.
list ()	Will result in a list.
locals ()	Will result in an updated dictionary of the current local symbol table.
map ()	Will result in the indicated iterator with the indicated function applied to each item.
max ()	Will result in the largest item of an iteration.
memoryview ()	Will result in memory view objects.
min ()	Will result in the smallest item of an iteration.
next ()	Will result in the next item in an iteration.
object ()	Will result in a new object.
oct ()	Converts a number into an octet.
open ()	Will open files and result in file objects.
ord ()	Conversion of an integer representing the Unicode of the indicated character.
pow ()	Will result in the value of a to the power of b.
print ()	Will print to the standard output device.
property ()	Will retrieve, set, and delete a property.

range ()	Will result in a sequence of numbers, beginning from 0 and default increments of 1.
repr ()	Will result in a readable version of objects.
reversed ()	Will result in a reversed iteration.
round ()	Rounding of a number.
set ()	Will result in new set objects.
setattr ()	Will set attributes of the objects.
slice ()	Will result in a sliced objects.
sorted ()	Will result in sorted lists.
staticmethod ()	Will convert methods into a static method.
str ()	Will result in string objects.
sum ()	Will sum the items of iterations.
super ()	Will result in an object representing the parent class.
tuple ()	Will result in tuples.
type ()	Will result in the type of objects.
vars ()	Will result in the _dict_ property of objects.
zip ()	Will result in a single iteration from multiple iterations.

Python Built-in String Methods

There are a number of built-in Python methods specifically for strings of data, which will result in new values for the string without making any changes to the original string. Here is a list of all such methods.

Method	Description
capitalize ()	Will convert the initial character to upper case.
casefold ()	Will convert strings into lower case.
center ()	Will result in centered strings.
count ()	Will result in the number of times an indicated value appears in a string.
encode ()	Will result in an encoded version of the strings.
endswith ()	Will result in true if the string ends with the indicated value.
expandtabs ()	Will set the tab size of the string.
find ()	Will search the string for indicated value and result in its position.
format ()	Will format indicated values of strings.
format_map ()	Will format indicated values of strings.
index ()	Will search the string for indicated value and result in its position.

isalnum ()	Will result in True if all string characters are alphanumeric.
isalpha ()	Will result in True if all string characters are alphabets.
isdecimal ()	Will result in True if all string characters are decimals.
isdigit ()	Will result in True if all string characters are digits.
isidentifier ()	Will result in True if the strings is an identifier.
islower ()	Will result in True if all string characters are lower case.
isnumeric ()	Will result in True if all string characters are numeric.
isprintable ()	Will result in True if all string characters are printable.
isspace ()	Will result in True if all string characters are whitespaces.
istitle ()	Will result in True if the string follows the rules of a title.
isupper ()	Will result in True if all string characters are upper case.
join ()	Will join the elements of an iteration to the end of the string.

ljust ()	Will result in a left-justified version of the string.
lower ()	Will convert a string into lower case.
lstrip ()	Will result in a left trim version of the string.
maketrans ()	Will result in a translation table to be used in translations.
partition ()	Will result in a tuple where the string is separated into 3 sections.
replace ()	Will result in a string where an indicated value is replaced with another indicated value.
rfind ()	Will search the string for an indicated value and result in its last position.
rindex ()	Will search the string for an indicated value and result in its last position.
rjust ()	Will result in the right justified version of the string.
rpartition ()	Will result in a tuple where the string is separated into 3 sections.
rsplit ()	Will split the string at the indicated separator and result in a list.
rstrip ()	Will result in a new string version that has been trimmed at its right.
split ()	Will split the string at the indicated separator and result in a list.

splitlines ()	Will split the string at line breaks and result in a list.
startswith ()	Will result in true if the string starts with the indicated value.
strip ()	Will result in a trimmed version of the string.
swapcase ()	Will swap the alphabet cases.
title ()	Will convert the first character of each word to upper case.
translate ()	Will result in a translated string.
upper ()	Will convert a string into upper case.
zfill ()	Will fill the string with the indicated number of 0 values at the beginning.

Python Random Numbers

A "random ()" function does not exist in Python, but it has an embedded module called "random" that may be utilized to create numbers randomly when needed. For instance, if you wanted to call the "random" module and display a number randomly between 100 and 500, you can accomplish this by executing the code below:

```python
import random

print (random.randrange (100, 500))
```

OUTPUT — Any number between 100 and 500 will be randomly displayed.

There are a number of defined methods in the random module as listed below:

Method	Description
betavariate ()	Will result in random float numbers between 0 and 1 based on the Beta distribution.
choice ()	Will result in random elements on the basis of the provided sequence.
choices ()	Will result in a list consisting of a random selection from the provided sequence.
expovariate ()	Will result in a float number randomly displayed between 0 and -1, or between 0 and 1 for negative parameters on the basis of the statistical exponential distributions.
gammavariate ()	Will result in a float number displayed between 0 and 1 on the basis of the statistical Gamma distribution.
gauss ()	Will result in a float number displayed between 0 and 1 on the basis of the Gaussian distribution, which is widely utilized in probability theory.
getrandbits ()	Will result in a number that represents the random bits.
getstate ()	Will result in the current internal state of the random number generator.

lognormvariate ()	Will result in a float number randomly displayed between 0 and 1 on the basis of a log-normal distribution, which is widely utilized in probability theory.
normalvariate()	Will result in a float number randomly displayed between 0 and 1 on the basis of the normal distribution, which is widely utilized in probability theory.
paretovariate()	Will result in a float number randomly displayed between 0 and 1 on the basis of the Pareto distribution, which is widely utilized in probability theory.
randint ()	Will result in a random number between the provided range.
random ()	Will result in a float number randomly displayed between 0 and 1.
randrange ()	Will result in a random number between the provided range.
sample ()	Will result in a sample of the sequences.
seed ()	Will trigger the random number generator.
setstate ()	Will restore the internal state of the random number generator.
shuffle ()	Will take a sequence and result in a sequence but in some random order.

triangular ()	Will result in a random float number between two provided parameters. You could also set a mode parameter for specification of the midpoint between the two other parameters.
uniform ()	Will result in a random float number between two provided parameters.
vonmisesvariate( )	Will result in a float number randomly displayed between 0 and 1 on the basis of the von "Mises distribution", which is utilized in directional statistics.
weibullvariate()	Will result in a float number randomly displayed between 0 and 1 on the basis of the Weibull distribution, which is utilized in statistics.

Python Built-in List methods

Python supports a number of built-in methods that can be used on lists or arrays, as listed in the table below:

Method	Description
append ()	Will insert an element at the end of the list.
clear ()	Will remove all the list elements.

copy ()	Will result in a replica of the list.
count ()	Will result in the number of elements with the indicated value.
extend ()	Will add the elements of a list (or any iterator), to the end of the current list.
index ()	Will result in the index of the first element with the indicated value.
insert ()	Will add an element at the indicated position.
pop ()	Will remove the element at the indicated position.
remove ()	Will remove the first item with the indicated value.
reverse ()	Will reverse the order of the list.
sort ()	Will sort the list.

Python Built-in Tuple Methods

Python supports a couple of built-in methods that can be used on tuples, as listed in the table below:

Method	Description
count ()	Will result in the number of times an indicated value appears in the tuple.
index ()	Will search a tuple for the indicated value and result in the position of where the value is found.

Python Built-in Set methods

Python also supports a variety of embedded methods that can be used on sets that are listed in the table below:

Method	Description
"add ()"	Will add an element to the set.
"clear ()"	Will remove all the elements from the set.
"copy ()"	Will result in a replica of the set.
"difference ()"	Will result in a set that contains the difference between 2 or more sets.

"difference_update ()"	Will remove the items from a set that can be found in another, indicated set.
"discard ()"	Will remove the indicated item.
"intersection ()"	Will result in a set that is the intersection of couple other sets.
"intersection_update ()"	Will remove the items from a set that are not present in another indicated set.
"isdisjoint ()"	Will determine if intersection exists between two sets.
"issubset ()"	Will determine if the identified set contains another set.
"issuperset ()"	Will determine if a different set contain the identified set or not.
"pop ()"	Will remove an element from the set.
"remove ()"	Will remove the indicated element.
"symmetric_difference ()"	Will result in a set with the symmetric differences of the two indicated sets.
"symmetric_difference_update ()"	Will insert the symmetric differences from the indicated set and other sets.
"union ()"	Will result in a set containing the union of sets.
"update ()"	Will update the set with the union of the inidcated set and other sets.

Python Built-in Dictionary Methods

Python also supports a large number of built-in methods that can be used on dictionaries that are listed in the table below:

Method	Description
clear ()	Will remove all the elements from the dictionary.
copy ()	Will result in a copy of the dictionary.
fromkeys ()	Will result in a dictionary with the indicated keys and values.
get ()	Will result in the values of the indicated key.
items ()	Will result in a list containing a tuple for every key-value pair.
keys ()	Will result in a list containing the keys of the dictionary.
pop ()	Will remove the elements with the indicated key.
popitem ()	Will remove the key value pair that was most recently added.
setdefault ()	Will result in the values of the indicated key. In case the key is not found, a new key will be added with the indicated values.
update ()	Will update the dictionary with the indicated key value pairs.

values ()	Will result in a list of all the values in the dictionary.

Python Built-in File Methods

Python also supports a large number of built-in methods that can be used on file objects that are listed in the table below:

Method	Description
close ()	Will close the file
detach ()	Will result in a separate raw stream.
fileno ()	Will result in a number representing the stream, per the operating system processing.
flush ()	Will flush the internal buffer.
isatty ()	Will result in determination if the file stream is interactive.
read ()	Will result in the content of the file.
readable ()	Will result in determination if the file stream is readable or not.
readline ()	Will result in one line from the file.
readlines ()	Will result in a list of lines from the file.
seek ()	Will modify the position of the file.

seekable ()	Will result in determination if the file permits modification of its position.
tell ()	Will result in the current position of the file.
truncate ()	Will change the size of the file to the indicated value.
writeable ()	Will result in determination if the file permits writing over.
write ()	Will write the indicated string to the file.
writelines ()	Will writes a list of strings to the file.

Python Keywords

Python contains some keywords that cannot be used to define a variable or used as a function name or any other unique identifier. These select Python keywords are listed in the table below:

Method	Description
"and"	Logical operator.
"as"	For creating an alias.
"assert"	To debug.
"break"	For breaking out of a loop.
"class"	For defining a class.

"continue"	For continuing to the next iteration of a loop.
"def"	For defining a function.
"del"	For deleting an object.
"elif"	For use in conditional statements, similar to "else if".
"else"	For use in conditional statements.
"except"	For use with exceptions, so the program knows the steps to follow in case of an exception.
"FALSE"	One of the data values assigned only to Boolean data type.
"finally"	For use with exceptions, this set of code would be executed regardless of any occurrences of an exception.
"for"	Used in creation of a "for loop".
"from"	For importing particular part of a module.
"global"	For declaring a global variable.
"if"	For making conditional statements.
"import"	For importing desired module.
"in"	For checking a specific data value within a tuple or a list.
"is"	For testing two variables that may be equal.
"lambda"	For creating an anonymous function.
"None"	For representation of null data value.
"nonlocal"	For declaration of a non-local variable.

"not"	Logical operator.
"or"	Logical operator.
"pass"	Will result in a null statement that would not be executed.
"raise"	Used to raise an exception to the statement.
"result in"	Used for exiting a function and resulting in a data value.
"TRUE"	One of the data values assigned only to Boolean data type.
"try"	Used for making "try except" statements.
"while"	For creating a "while loop".
"with"	Used for simplification of the handling procedure for exceptions.
"yield"	For terminating a function and resulting in a generator.

Python is widely used for a large variety of web-based projects spanning across the industrial spectrum. In the last chapter, you learned about the development of websites and web based applications using a Python-based data framework. Python is widely used in the development and testing of software programs, machine learning algorithms and Artificial Intelligence technologies to solve real world problems. The science of developing human controlled and operated machinery, such as digital computers or robots, that can mimic human intelligence, adapt to new inputs, and perform human like tasks is called "Artificial Intelligence" or AI. Let's look at real life applications of the Python programming language in different arenas of the modern life. Some of the widely used web frameworks such as "Django" and "Flask" have been developed using Python. These frameworks assist the developer in writing server-side codes that enable management of database, generation of backend programming logic, mapping of URL, among others.

A variety of machine learning models have been written exclusively in Python. Machine learning is a way for machines to write logic in order to learn and fix a specific issue on its own. For instance, Python-based machine learning algorithms used in the development of "product recommendation systems" for eCommerce businesses such as Amazon, Netflix, YouTube, and many more. Other instances of Python-based machine learning models are facial recognition and the voice recognition technologies available on our mobile devices. Python can also be used in the development of data visualization and data analysis tools and techniques such as scatter plots and other graphical representations of data. "Scripting" can be defined as the process of generating simple programs for automation of straightforward tasks like those required to send automated email responses and text messages. You could develop these types of software using the Python programming language. A wide variety of gaming programs have been developed with the use of Python.

Python also supports the development of "embedded applications." You could use data libraries such as "TKinter" or "QT" to create desktop apps based on Python.

Gaming Industry

Python based artificial intelligence programs are at the heart of the gaming industry, with its groundbreaking simulation and virtual experience technologies. In 1949, mathematician Claude Shannon developed a 'one player chess game' using the rudimentary Machine learning algorithms, where people would compete against a computer instead of another person. In 1989, the "Sim City" game successfully stimulated realistic and deeply human characteristics like unpredictability, with its use of artificial intelligence technology. In 2000, the "Total War" game incorporated human like emotions into their virtual fighters mimicking the soldiers in real-life battlefields.

In 2017, the leading gaming company, Electronic Arts, announced establishment of their new research and development division called "SEED". This division is dedicated solely to the exploration of artificial intelligence based technologies and creative opportunities for future giving products. Another billion-dollar gaming company called Epic Games collaborated with CubicMotion, 3Lateral, Tencent, and Vicon to develop in realistic virtual human named

"Siren," marking a tremendous step forward in gaming as well as the film industry.

Cost Saving

Since the early 1980s, procedural content generation has become an area of grave importance for game development. This pertains to the generation of game levels and rules, quest and stories, spatial maps, Music and props such as vehicles, weapons and powers as well as Game characters. This is gaming content creation; it's traditionally done by highly skilled Game artists and developers that tend to be expensive and in high demand. The development of a single game requires hundreds of people working for several years adding to the high cost of game development. Consequently, the gaming industry is enticed by the lucrative artificial intelligence technology to create high-quality gaming content at a fraction of the cost.

In 2018, Nivdia collaborated with an independent game development company called Remedy Entertainment to develop an automated real-time deep learning Technology that can create three-dimensional facial animations from audio. This technology will be useful in the development of low cost localization, in-game dialogue, and virtual reality avatars. In 2019, Italy's Politecnico di Milano launched a game level-design artificial intelligence using generative adversarial networks (GANs), which is a deep neutral network composed of two nets contested within each other. A popular first person shooter video game called "DOOM" now contains maps designed using this technology.

Enhancing Gaming Experience

The gaming industry is leveraging artificial intelligence Technology to understand what players do and how they feel during the play in order to be able to model a human player. To gauge and build models of player experience, supervised machine learning Technologies such as "Artificial Neural Networks" and "Support Vector Machines" are used. Select aspects of the game and player-game interaction serve as the training data resources. For example, the video game "Grand Theft Auto" is being used and the development off autonomous vehicles by training them to recognize stop signs. Another example of gaming technology being leveraged by AI researchers to aid in machine learning is the sandbox video game "Minecraft," which enables players to construct a virtual 3-D world using a variety of building blocks.

Automation and Personalization of Customer Service With Chatbots

With the advancements in the natural language processing technology, the consumers' ability to distinguish between the human voice and the voice of a robot is increasingly diminishing. Chatbots, with their more human like voices and ability to resolve customer issues independently and in the absence of human assistance, are the future of customer service, and it's bound to expand from banking to all other industries. The banks will soon be reporting huge savings and significant cost reductions in the next 10 years. A recent study predicted up to $450 billion in savings by the banking and lending industry by 2030.

Despite this huge promise and reward brought on by AI powered Chatbots, banking and other industries need to tread with caution when it comes to delivering service that meets or succeeds customer expectations. The reality is humans today, and for the foreseeable future, like to speak with another person to address and resolve their issues. The nuances of human problems seem too far-fetched to be understood by a callus robot. The best approach seems to be human customer service representatives augmented by the Chatbots rather than replacing humans completely. For example, the renowned Swiss bank UBS, with a global ranking of 35 for the volume of its assets, has partnered with Amazon. Amazon has successfully incorporated a "Ask UBS" service on their AI powered speakers called Amazon Echo (Alexa). UBS customers across the world can simply "ask" Alexa for advice and analysis on global financial markets in lieu of The Wall Street Journal. The "Ask UBS" service is also designed to offer definitions and examples for the finance related jargon and acronyms. However, "Ask UBS" application is unable to offer personalized advice to the UBS clients, owing to a lack of access to individual portfolios and client's holding and goals. This inability stems from security and privacy concerns regarding client data.

With the wealth of customer data including records of online and offline transactions and detailed demographics, banking industry is sitting on a gold mine that needs the power of AI based analytics to dig out the gold with data mining. Integration and analysis of information sourced from discrete databases has uniquely positioned banks to utilize Machine learning and obtain a complete view of their customers' needs and provide superior personalized services.

> *"The next step within the digital service model is for banks to price for the individual, and to negotiate that price in real time, taking personalization to the ultimate level."*
>
> *– James Eardley, SAP Marketing Director*

For all the financial institutions, customer personalization has transcended from marketing and product customization into the realm of cybersecurity. Biometric data, like fingerprints, is increasingly being used to augment or replace traditional passwords and other means of identity verification. A recent study by "Google Intelligence" reported that by 2021 about 2 billion bank customers will be using some or other form of biometric identification. One of the leading tech giants, Apple, has descended onto payment platform and is now using their Artificial Intelligence powered "facial recognition technology" to unlock their devices and also to validate payments, using their "digital wallet" service called "Apple Pay."

Healthcare Applications

- AI-assisted robotic surgery – The biggest draw of robot assisted surgery is that they do not require large incisions and are considered minimally invasive with low post-op recovery time. Robots are capable of analyzing data from pre-op patient medical records and subsequently guiding the surgeon's instruments during surgery. These robot-assisted surgeries have reported up to a 21% reduction in patients' hospital stays. Robots can also use data from past surgeries and use AI to inform the surgeon about any new possible techniques. The most advanced surgical robot, "Da Vinci," allows surgeons to carry out complex surgical procedures with higher accuracy and greater control than the conventional methods.

- Supplement clinical diagnosis – Although the use of AI in diagnostics is still under the radar, a lot of successful use cases have already been reported. An algorithm created at

Stanford University is capable of detecting skin cancer with similar competencies as that of a skilled dermatologist. An AI software program in Denmark was used to eavesdrop on emergency phone calls made to human dispatchers. The underlying algorithm analyzed the tone and words of the caller as well as the background noise to detect cases of heart attack. The AI program had a 93% success rate, which was 20% higher than the human counterparts.

- Virtual Nursing Assistants – The virtual nurses are available 24*7 without fatigue and lapse in judgment. They provide constant patient monitoring and directions for the most effective care while answering all of the patient's questions quickly and efficiently. An increase in regular communication between patients and their care providers can be credited to virtual nursing applications. This prevents unnecessary hospital visits and readmission. The virtual nurse assistant at Care Angel can already provide wellness checks through Artificial Intelligence and voice.

- Automation of administrative tasks – AI driven technology such as voice to text transcriptions are aiding in ordering test, prescribing medications, and even writing medical chart notes. The partnership between IBM and Cleveland Clinic has allowed IBM's Watson to perform mining on clinical health data and help physicians in developing personalized and more efficient treatment plans.

Finance Sector

Fraud Prevention

The inherent capability of Artificial Intelligence to swiftly analyze large volumes of data and identify patterns that may not come naturally to the human observer has made AI the smoking gun for fraud detection and prevention. According to a recent report by McAfee global economy suffered a $600 billion loss through cybercrime alone. Real time fraud detection is the only direct path to prevent fraud from happening in the first place. AI and machine learning based solutions are empowering financial service providers with real time fraud detection as well as reducing the frequency of legitimate transactions being flagged as fraudulent. The MasterCard company has reported an 80% decline in the legitimate activity being marked as "false fraud," with its use of Artificial Intelligence technology.

Lending Risk Management

Banks and other money lending institutions bear high risk while giving out loans to the borrowers. This complex process of underwriting requires accuracy and high confidentiality. This is where AI swoops in to save the day by analyzing available transaction data, market trends, and recent financial activities pertinent to the prospective borrower and assessing potential risks in approving the loan(s).

Hedge Fund Management

Today, over $3 trillion in assets of the world economy are managed by hedge funds. The investment partnerships between investors or "limited partners" and professional fund managers are called hedge funds. Hedge fund's strategy to minimize the risk and maximize returns for the investors dictates the contribution made by the "limited partner" and the management of those funds by the general partner. The hedge funds epitomize the idiom "bigger the risk, bigger the reward" and are considered riskier investments. The hedge fund managers are responsible for shorting their stocks if they anticipate the market will drop or "hedge" by going long when they anticipate the market will grow. This stock trading can soon be taken over Artificial Intelligence based solutions requiring no human intervention and revolutionize the hedge fund management.

The ability of Artificial Intelligence powered machines to analyze massive amounts of data in a fraction of time. Then it takes a human and gather insight from its analysis to self-learn and improve its trading acumen is indeed a big winner. As intriguing as the use of AI to trade stocks appears, it is still missing the proof of concept, but nevertheless, companies are continuing to research and develop AI powered systems that could potentially kick start a new era on Wall Street.

Transportation Industry

The transportation industry is highly susceptible two problems arising from human errors, traffic, and accidents. These problems are too difficult to model owing to their inherently unpredictable nature but can be easily overcome with the use of Artificial Intelligence powered tools that can analyze observed data and make or predict the appropriate decisions. The challenge of increasing travel demand, safety concerns, CO2 emissions, and environmental degradation can be met with the power of artificial intelligence. From Artificial Neural Networks to Bee colony optimization, a whole lot of artificial intelligence techniques are being employed to make the transportation industry efficient and effective. To obtain significant relief from traffic congestion while making travel time more reliable for the population, transport authorities are experimenting with a variety of AI based solutions. With potential application of artificial intelligence for enhanced road infrastructure and assistance for drivers, the transportation industry it's focused on accomplishing a more reliable transport system, which will have limited to no effect on the environment while being cost effective.

It is an uphill battle to fully understand the relationships between the characteristics of various transportation systems using the traditional methods. Artificial intelligence is here once again to offer the panacea by transforming the traffic sensors on the road into a smart agent that can potentially detect accidents and predict the future traffic conditions. Rapid development has been observed in the area of Intelligent Transport Systems (ITS), which are targeted to alleviate traffic congestion and improve driving experience by utilizing multiple Technologies and communication systems. They are capable of collecting and storing data that can be easily integrated with machine learning technology. To increase the efficiency of police patrol and keeping the citizens of safe collection of crime data is critical and can be achieved with the right AI powered tools. Artificial intelligence can also simplify the transportation planning of the road freight transport system by providing accurate prediction methods to forecast their volume.

Here are some real world examples of artificial intelligence being used in the transportation industry:

- Local motors company, in collaboration with IBM's Watson, has unveiled an AI powered autonomous fully electric vehicle called "Olli."

- A highly promising traffic control system developed by Rapid Flow Technologies is called "SURTRAC," which allows traffic lights at intersections to respond to vehicular flow on an individual level instead of being a part of a centralized system.A Chinese company called "TuSimple" entered the American market with their self-driving trucks that can utilize long distance sensors with a complete observation range and it's deep learning artificial intelligence technology allows seamless detection and tracking of objects using multiple cameras.

- Rolls-Royce is expected to launch air own clueless cargo ships by 2020 that could be controlled remotely and pioneer the way for fully autonomous ships in the near future.In early 2019, the first autonomous trains were tested by the London underground train system that can potentially carry more passengers in lieu of driver's cabin.

- Some commuters in Sweden have reportedly been testing microchip implants on their body as travel tickets.

- China launched the Autonomous Rail Rapid Transit System (ART) in the city of Zhuzhou that doesn't require tracks, and instead, the trains follow the virtual track created by painted dashed lines.Autonomous delivery trucks could soon be bringing our food and mail to us instead of the human driven delivery service.

- Dubai is experimenting with Smart technology driven digital number plates for cars, which can immediately send an alert to the authorities in the event of an accident.

- Some of the American airports are you using artificial intelligence a face scanning technologies to verify the identities of passengers before allowing them to board the flight and ditching the traditional passports.

- The revolutionizing Google flights technology is able to predict flight delays before the airlines themselves by using Advanced machine learning technology on the available data from previous flights and providing passengers a more accurate expected time of arrival.

- When it comes to real-time customer service, the Trainline app has surpassed all AI powered applications on the market, with its BusyBot technology that can help the passengers with there change tickets booking and purchase as well as find a vacant seat on the train in real-time. This bot collects information from the passengers on board on how busy their carriages are and then analyzes that data to advise other passengers on potentially vacant seating.

- The "JOZU" app is aimed at once again liberating the modern woman who likes to travel alone and is concerned about her safety. It collects user data to provide women with the safest routes and methods of transport.

- China has pioneered the development of a smart highway that can charge electric vehicles as they are driving, and Australia is set to follow the lead. Smart roads are being designed to incorporate sensors to monitor traffic patterns and solar panels for vehicle charging.

- Smart luggage with built-in GPS tracker and weighing scales connected to your phones are already available on the market.

- Ford has recently announced its plan to file a patent for their Artificial Intelligence based unmanned "Robotic Police Car" that can issue tickets for speeding and other violations to drivers by scanning their car registration and accessing the CCTV footage.

- Japan will soon be enjoying a new ride-hailing service. Sony recently announced the launch of their new service that will use Artificial Intelligence to manage fleets and provide an overview of potential traffic issues like congestions and detours due to public events.

- Ford has designed a "Smart City" with the system that allows smart vehicles to connect and coordinate with one another while cutting down on the risks of collisions and other accidents. The Smart city would collect data from its residents and share it with multiple smart technologies working in tandem to create a digital utopia.

CHAPTER 3

Data Analysis and Mining With Python

In 2001, Gartner defined Big data as "Data that contains greater variety arriving in increasing volumes and with ever-higher velocity." This led to the formulation of the "three V's." Big data refers to an avalanche of structured and unstructured data that is endlessly flooding and from a variety of endless data sources. These data sets are too large to be analyzed with traditional analytical tools and technologies but have a plethora of valuable insights hiding underneath.

The "Vs" of Big Data

Volume – To be classified as big data, the volume of the given data set must be substantially larger than traditional data sets. These data sets are primarily composed of unstructured data with limited structured and semi structured data. The unstructured data or the data with unknown value can be collected from input sources such as webpages, search history, mobile applications, and social media platforms. The size and customer base of the company is usually proportional to the volume of the data acquired by the company.

Velocity – The speed at which data can be gathered and acted upon the first to the velocity of big data. Companies are increasingly using a combination of on-premise and cloud-based servers to increase the speed of their data collection. The modern-day "Smart Products and Devices" require real-time access to consumer data, in order to be able to provide them a more engaging and enhanced user experience.

Variety – Traditionally a data set would contain majority of structured data with low volume of unstructured and semi-structured data, but the advent of big data has given rise to new unstructured data types such as video, text, audio that require sophisticated tools and technologies to clean and process these data types to extract meaningful insights from them.

Veracity – Another "V" that must be considered for big data analysis is veracity. This refers to the "trustworthiness or the quality" of the data. For example, social media platforms like Facebook and Twitter with blogs and posts containing hashtags, acronyms, and all kinds of typing errors can significantly reduce the reliability and accuracy of the data sets.

Value – Data has evolved as a currency of its own with intrinsic value. Just like traditional monetary currencies, the ultimate value of the big data is directly proportional to the insight gathered from it.

History of Big Data

The origin of large volumes of data can be traced back to the 1960s and 1970s when the Third Industrial Revolution had just started to kick in, and the development of relational databases had begun along with the construction of data centers. But the concept of big data has recently taken center stage primarily since the availability of free search engines like Google and Yahoo, free online entertainment services like YouTube and social media platforms like Facebook. In 2005, businesses started to recognize the incredible amount of user data being generated through these platforms and services, and in the same year and open-source framework called "Hadoop," was developed to gather and analyze these large data dumps available to the companies. During the same period, non-relational or distributed database called "NoSQL" started to gain popularity due to its ability to store and extract unstructured data. "Hadoop" made it possible for the companies to work with big data with high ease and at a relatively low cost.

Today with the rise of cutting edge technology, not only humans but machines also generating data. The smart device technologies like

"Internet of things" (IoT) and "Internet of systems" (IoS) have skyrocketed the volume of big data. Our everyday household objects and smart devices are connected to the Internet and able to track and record our usage patterns as well as our interactions with these products and feeds all this data directly into the big data. The advent of machine learning technology has further increased the volume of data generated on a daily basis. It is estimated that by 2020, "1.7 MB of data will be generated per second per person." As the big data will continue to grow, it usability still has many horizons to cross.

Importance of Big Data

To gain reliable and trustworthy information from a data set, it is very important to have a complete data set that has been made possible with the use of big data technology. The more data we have, the more information and details can be extracted out of it. To gain a 360 view of a problem, and its underlying solutions, the future of big data is very promising. Here are some examples of the use of big data:

Product development – Large and small e-commerce businesses are increasingly relying upon big data to understand customer demands and expectations. Companies can develop predictive models to launch new products and services by using primary characteristics of their past and existing products and services and generating a model describing the relationship of those characteristics with the commercial success of those products and services. For example, a leading fast manufacturing commercial goods company Procter & Gamble, extensively uses big data gathered from the social media websites, test markets, and focus groups in preparation for their new product launch.

Predictive maintenance – In order to besides leave project potential mechanical and equipment failures, a large volume of unstructured data such as error messages, log entries, and normal temperature of the machine must be analyzed along with available structured data such as make and model of the equipment and year of manufacturing. By analyzing this big data set using the required analytical tools, companies can extend the shelf life of their equipment by preparing for scheduled maintenance ahead of time and predicting future occurrences of potential mechanical failures.

Customer experience – The smart customer is aware of all of the technological advancements and is loyal only to the most engaging and enhanced user experience available. This has triggered a race among the companies to provide unique customer experiences analyzing the data gathered from customers' interactions with the company's products and services. Providing personalized recommendations and offers to reduce customer churn rate and effectively kind words prospective leads into paying customers.

Fraud and compliance – Big data helps in identifying the data patterns and assessing historical trends from previous fraudulent transactions to effectively detect and prevent potentially fraudulent transactions. Banks, financial institutions, and online payment services like PayPal are constantly monitoring and gathering customer transaction data in an effort to prevent fraud.

Operational efficiency – With the help of big data predictive analysis. companies can learn and anticipate future demand and product trends by analyzing production capacity, customer feedback, and data pertaining to top-selling items and product Will result in to improve decision-making and produce products that are in line with the current market trends.

Machine learning – For a machine to be able to learn and train on its own, it requires a humongous volume of data, i.e., big data. A solid training set containing structured, semi-structured, and unstructured data will help the machine to develop a multidimensional view of the real world and the problem it is engineered to resolve. (Details on machine learning will be provided later in this book.)

Drive innovation – By studying and understanding the relationships between humans and their electronic devices as well as the manufacturers of these devices, companies can develop improved and innovative products by examining current product trends and meeting customer expectations.

The Functioning of Big Data

There are three important actions required to gain insights from big data:

Integration – The traditional data integration methods such as ETL (Extract, Transform, Load) are incapable of collating data from a wide variety of unrelated sources and applications that are you at the heart of big data. Advanced tools and technologies are required to analyze big data sets that are exponentially larger than traditional data sets. By integrating big data from these disparate sources, companies are able to analyze and extract valuable insight to grow and maintain their businesses.

Management – Big data management can be defined as "the organization, administration, and governance of large volumes of both structured and unstructured data." Big data requires efficient and cheap storage, which can be accomplished using servers that are on-premise, cloud-based, or a combination of both. Companies are able to seamlessly access required data from anywhere across the world, and then processing this is data using required processing engines on an as-needed basis. The goal is to make sure the quality of the data is high-level and can be accessed easily by the required tools and applications. Big data gathered from all kinds of Dale sources including social media platforms, search engine history and call logs. The big data usually contains large sets of unstructured data and semi-structured data, which are stored in a variety of formats. To be able to process and store this complicated data, companies require more powerful and advanced data management software beyond the traditional relational databases and data warehouse platforms.

New platforms are available in the market that are capable of combining big data with the traditional data warehouse systems in a "logical data warehousing architecture." As part of this effort, companies are required to make decisions on what data must be secured for regulatory purposes and compliance, what data must be kept for future analytical purposes, and what data has no future use and can be disposed of. This process is called "data classification," which allows rapid and efficient analysis of the subset of data to be included in the immediate decision-making process of the company.

Analysis – Once the big data has been collected and is easily accessible, it can be analyzed using advanced analytical tools and technologies. This analysis will provide valuable insight and actionable information. Big data can be explored to make new discoveries and develop data models using artificial intelligence and machine learning algorithms.

Data Mining

Data mining can be defined as "the process of exploring and analyzing large volumes of data to gather meaningful patterns and rules." Data mining falls under the umbrella of data science and is heavily used to build artificial intelligence based machine learning models, for example, search engine algorithms. Although the process of "digging through data" to uncover hidden patterns and predict future events has been around for a long time and referred to as "knowledge discovery in databases," the term "Data mining" was coined as recently as the 1990s.

Data mining consists of three foundational and highly intertwined disciplines of science, namely, "statistics" (the mathematical study of data relationships), "machine learning algorithms" (algorithms that can be trained with an inherent capability to learn) and "artificial intelligence" (machines that can display human-like intelligence). With the advent of big data, Data mining technology has been evolved to keep up with the "limitless potential of big data" and affordable computing power. The once considered tedious, labor-intensive, and time consuming activities have been automated using advance processing speed and power of the modern computing systems.

"Data mining is the process of finding anomalies, patterns, and correlations within large data sets to predict outcomes. Using a broad range of techniques, you can use this information to increase revenues, cut costs, improve customer relationships, reduce risks, and more."

– SAS

According to SAS, "unstructured data alone makes up 90% of the digital universe". This avalanche of big data does not necessarily guarantee more knowledge. The application of data mining technology allows the filtering of all the redundant and unnecessary data noise to garner the understanding of relevant information that can be used in the immediate decision-making process.

Applications of Data Mining

The applications of data mining technology are far and wide, ranging from retail pricing and promotions to credit risk assessment by financial institutions and banks. Every industrial sector is benefiting from the applications the data mining technology. Here are some of the examples of industrial applications and data mind technology:

Healthcare Bio-Informatics

To predict the likelihood of the patient suffering from one or more health conditions given the risk factors, statistical models are used by healthcare professionals. Genetically transferred diseases can be prevented or mediated from the onset of deteriorating health condition, by modeling the patient's genetic, family, and demographic data. In developing nations there is a scarcity of healthcare professionals, therefore, assisted diagnoses and prioritization of patients is very critical. Data mining based models have recently been deployed in such countries to help with the prioritization of patients before healthcare professionals can reach these countries and administer treatment.

Credit Risk Management

Financial institutions and banks deploy data mining models tools to predict the likelihood of a potential credit card customer failing to make their credit payments on time as well as to determine appropriate credit limit that the customer may qualify for. These data mining models collect and extract information from a variety of input sources including personal information, Financial history of the customer at and demographic among other sources. The model then provides the institution or bank interest rate to be collected from the client based on the assessed risk. For example, Data mining models take the credit score of the applicant into consideration and individuals with a low Credit score are given the high interest rates.

Spam Filtering

A lot of email clients such as "Google mail" and "Yahoo mail" rely on the data mining tools to detect and flag email spam and malware. By analyzing hundreds and thousands of shared characteristics of spams and malware, the data mining tool provides insight that can be used in the development of enhanced security measures and tools. These applications are not only capable of detecting spam, but they are also very efficient in categorizing the spam emails and storing them in a separate folder, so they never enter the user's inbox.

Marketing

Retail companies have an incessant need to understand their customer demands and expectations. With the use of data mining tools, businesses can analyze customer related data such as purchase history, demographics, gender, and age to gather valuable customer insights and segment them into groups based on shared shopping attributes. Companies then devise unique marketing strategies and campaigns to target specific groups such as discount offers and promotions.

Sentiment Analysis

With the use of a technique called "text mining," companies can analyze their data from all of their social media platforms to understand the "sentiment" of their customer base. This process of understanding the feelings of a big group of people towards a particular topic is called "sentiment analysis" and can be carried out using data mining tools. With the use of pattern recognition technology, input data from social media platforms and other related public content websites are collected using the "text mining" technology and identify data patterns that feed into a general understanding of the topic. To further dive into this data, the "natural language processing" technique can be used to understand the human language in a specific context.

Qualitative Data Mining

The "text mining" technique can also be used to perform quantitative research and gain insight from large volumes of unstructured data. Recently a research study conducted by the University of Berkeley revealed the use of data mining models and child welfare program studies.

Product Recommendation Systems

Advance "recommendations systems" are like the bread and butter for online retailers. The use of predictive customer behavior analysis is rising among small and large online businesses to gain a competitive edge in the market. Some of the largest e-commerce businesses including "Amazon," Macy's," and" Nordstrom," have invested millions of dollars in the development of their own proprietary data mining models to forecast market trends and all for a more engaging in enhanced user experience to their customers. The on-demand entertainment giant "Netflix" bought over a million dollars' worth algorithm to enhance the accuracy of their video recommendation system, which reportedly increased the recommendation accuracy for "Netflix" by over 8%.

The Data Mining Process

Most widely used data mining processes can be broken down into six steps as listed below:

1. Business understanding

It is very critical to understand the project goals and what is it that you're trying to achieve through the data mining process. Companies always start with the establishment of a defined goal and a project plan that includes details such as individual team member roles and responsibility, project milestones, project timelines and key performance indicators and metrics.

2. Data understanding

Data is available from a wide variety of input sources and in different formats. With the use of data visualization tools, the data properties and features can be assessed to ensure the existing data set is able to meet the established business requirements and project goals.

3. Data preparation

The preprocessing of Data collected in multiple formats is very important. The data set must be scrubbed to remove data redundancies and identify gaps before it is deemed appropriate for mining. Considering the amount of data to be analyzed, the data pre-processing and processing steps can take a long time. To enhance the speed of the data mining process, instead of using a single system companies prefer using distributed systems as part of their "database management systems." The distributed systems also provide enhanced security measures by segregating the data into multiple devices rather than a single data warehouse. At this stage, it is also very crucial to account for backup options and failsafe measures in the event of data loss during the data manipulation stage.

4. Data modeling

Applicable mathematical models and analytical tools are applied to the data set to identify patterns.

5. Evaluation

The modeling results and data patterns are evaluating against the project goal and objectives to determine if the data findings can be released for use across the organization.

6. Deployment

Once the insights gathered from the data has been evaluated as applicable to the functioning and operations of the organization, these insights can be shared across the company to be included in its day-to-day operations. With the use of a Business Intelligence tool, the data findings can be stored at a centralized location and accessed using the BI tool as needed.

Pros of Data Mining

Automated Decision-Making

With the use of data mining technology, businesses can seamlessly automate tedious manual tasks and analyze large volumes of data to gather insights for the routine and critical decision-making processes. For example, financial lending institutions, banks and online payment services use data mining technology to detect potentially fraudulent transactions, verify user identity and ensure data privacy to protect their customers against identity theft. When a company's operational algorithms are working in coordination with the data mining models, a company can independently gather, analyze and take actions on data to improve and streamline their operational decision-making process.

Accurate Prediction and Forecasting

Project planning is fundamental to the success of any company. Managers and executives can leverage data mining technology to gather reliable forecasts and predictions on future market trends and include in their future planning process. For example, one of the leading retail company "Macy's" has implemented demand forecasting models to generate reliable demand forecasts for Mary is clothing categories at individual stores, in order to increase the efficiency of their supply chain by routing the forecasted inventory to each store and cater to the needs of the market more efficiently.

Cost Reduction

With the help of data mining technologies, companies can maximize the use of their resources by smarty allocating them across the business model. The use of data mining technology in planning, as well as an automated decision-making process, results in accurate forecasts leading to significant cost reductions. For example, a major airline company "Delta" implemented RFID chips inside their passengers checked in baggage and gathered baggage handling data that was analyzed using data mining technology to identify improvement opportunities in their process and minimizing the number of mishandled baggage. This not only resulted in cost saving on the search and rerouting process of the lost baggage but also translated into higher customer satisfaction.

Customer Insights

Companies across different industrial sectors have deployed Data mining models to gather valuable insights from existing customer data, which can be used to segment and target customers with similar shopping attributes using similar marketing strategies and campaigns. Customer personas can be created using data mining technology to provide a more engaging and personalized user experience to the customer. For example, "Disney" has recently invested over billion dollars in developing and deploying "Magic bands," offering the convenience and enhanced experience and Disney resorts. At the same time, these bands can be used to collect data on patron activities and interactions with different "Disney" products and services at the park to further enhance the "Disney experience."

"When [data mining and] predictive analytics are done right, the analyses aren't a means to a predictive end; rather, the desired predictions become a means to analytical insight and discovery. We do a better job of analyzing what we really need to analyze and predicting what we really want to predict."

– Harvard Business Review Insight Center Report

Challenges of Data Mining

1. Big data

Our digital life has inundated companies with large volumes of data which is estimated to reach 1.7 MB per second per person by 2020. This exponential increase in volume and complexity of big data has presented challenges for the data mining technology. Companies are looking to expedite their decision-making process by swiftly and efficiently extracting and analyzing data to gain valuable insights from their data treasure trove. The ultimate goal of data mining technology is to overcome these challenges and unlock the true potential of data value. The "4Vs" of big data namely velocity, variety, volume and veracity, represent the four major challenges facing the data mining technology.

The skyrocketing "velocity" or speed at which new data is being generated poses a challenge of increasing storage requirements. The "variety" or different data types collected and stored require advance data mining capabilities to be able to simultaneously process a multitude of data formats. Data mining tools that are not equipped to process such highly variable big data provide low value, due to their inefficiency and analyzing unstructured and structured data together.

The large volume of big data is not only challenging for storage but it's even more challenging do identify correct data in a timely manner, owing to a massive reduction in the speed of the data mining tools and algorithms. To add on to this challenge, the data "veracity" denoting that all of the collected data is not accurate and can be incomplete or even biased. The data mining tools are struggling to deliver high-quality results in a timely manner by analyzing high quantity or big data.

2. Overloading models

Data models that describe the natural errors of the data set instead of the underlying patterns are often "over-fitted" or overloaded. These models tend to be highly complex and the choir, a large number of independent media, bowls to precisely predict a future event. Data volume and variety further increase the risk of overloading. A high number of variables tend to restrict the data model within the confines of the known sample data. On the other hand, an insufficient number of variables can compromise the relevance of the model. To obtain the required number of variables for the data mining models, to be able to strike a balance between the accuracy of the results and the prediction capabilities is one of the major challenges facing the data mining technology today.

3. Data privacy and security

To cater to the large volume of big data generated on a daily basis, companies are investing in cloud based storage servers along with its on premise servers. The cloud computing technology is relatively new in the market and the inherent nature of this service poses multiple security and privacy concerns. Data privacy and security is one of the biggest concerns of Smart consumers who are willing to take their business to the company that can promise them the security of their personal information and data. This requires organizations to evaluate their customer relationship and prioritize customer privacy over the development of policies that can potentially compromise customer data security.

4. Scaling costs

With the increasing speed of data generation leading to a high volume of complex data, organizations are required to expand their data mining models and deploy them across the organization. To unlock the full potential of data mining tools, companies are required to heavily invest in computing infrastructure and processing power to efficiently run the data mining models. Big ticket item purchase including data servers, software, and advance computers, must be made in order to scale the analytical capabilities of the organization.

Machine Learning Libraries

Machine learning libraries are sensitive routines and functions that are written in any given language. Software developers require a robust set of libraries to perform complex tasks without needing to rewrite multiple lines of code. Machine learning is largely based on mathematical optimization, probability, and statistics.

Python is the language of choice in the field of machine learning credited to consistent development time and flexibility. It is well suited to develop sophisticated models and production engines that can be directly plugged into production systems. One of its greatest assets being an extensive set of libraries that can help researchers who are less equipped with developer knowledge to easily execute machine learning.

"Scikit-Learn" has evolved as the gold standard for machine learning using Python, offering a wide variety of "supervised" and "unsupervised" ML algorithms. It is touted as one of the most user friendly and cleanest machine learning libraries to date. For example, decision trees, clustering, linear and logistics regressions, and K-means. Scikit-learn uses a couple of basic Python libraries: NumPy and SciPy and adds a set of algorithms for data mining tasks, including classification, regression and clustering. It is also capable of implementing tasks like feature selection, transforming data and ensemble methods in only a few lines.

In 2007, David Cournapeau, developed the foundational code of "Scikit-Learn" as part of a "Summer of Code" project for "Google." Scikit-learn has become one of Python's most famous open source machine learning libraries since its launch in 2007. But it wasn't until 2010 that Scikit-Learn was released for public use. Scikit-Learn is an open sourced and BSD licensed data mining and data analysis tool used to develop supervise, and unsupervised machine learning algorithms build on Python. Scikit-learn offers various ML algorithms such as "classification," "regression," "dimensionality reduction," and "clustering." It also offers modules for feature extraction, data processing, and model evaluation.

Designed as an extension to the "SciPy" library, Scikit-Learn is based on "NumPy" and "Matplotlib," the most popular Python libraries. NumPy expands Python to support efficient operations on big arrays and multidimensional matrices. Matplotlib offers visualization tools and science computing modules are provided by SciPy. For scholarly studies, Scikit-Learn is popular because it has a well-documented, easy-to-use and flexible API. Developers are able to utilize Scikit-Learn for their experiments with various algorithms by only altering a few lines of the code. Scikit-Learn also provides a variety of training datasets, enabling developers to focus on algorithms instead of data collection and cleaning. Many of the algorithms of Scikit-Learn are quick and scalable to all but huge datasets. Scikit-learn is known for its reliability, and automated tests are available for much of the library. Scikit-learn is extremely popular with beginners in machine learning to start implementing simple algorithms.

Prerequisites for Application of Scikit-Learn Library

The Scikit-Learn library is based on the SciPy (Scientific Python), which needs to be installed before using SciKit-Learn. This stack involves the following:

NumPy (Base n-dimensional Array Package)

"NumPy" is the basic package with Python to perform scientific computations. It includes, among other things: "a powerful N-dimensional array object; sophisticated (broadcasting) functions; tools for integrating C/C++ and Fortran code; useful linear algebra, Fourier transform, and random number capabilities." NumPy is widely reckoned as an effective multi-dimensional container of generic data in addition to its apparent scientific uses. It is possible to define arbitrary data types. This enables NumPy to integrate with a broad variety of databases seamlessly and quickly. The primary objective of NumPy is the homogeneity of multidimensional array. It consists of an element table (generally numbers), all of which are of the same sort and are indicated by tuples of non-negative integers. The dimensions of NumPy are called "axes," and array class is called "ndarray."

Matplotlib (Comprehensive 2D/3D Plotting)

"Matplotlib" is a 2 dimensional graphic generation library from Python that produces high quality numbers across a range of hardcopy formats and interactive environments. The "Python script," the "Python," "IPython shells," the "Jupyter notebook," the web app servers, and select user interface toolkits can be used with Matplotlib. Matplotlib attempts to further simplify easy tasks and make difficult tasks feasible. With only a few lines of code, you can produce tracks, histograms, scatter plots, bar graphs, error graphs, etc.

A MATLAB-like interface is provided for easy plotting of the Pyplot Module, especially when coupled with IPython. As a power user, you can regulate the entire line styles, fonts properties and axis properties through an object-oriented interface or through a collection of features similar to the one provided to MATLAB users.

SciPy (Fundamental Library for Scientific Computing)

SciPy is a "collection of mathematical algorithms and convenience functions built on the NumPy extension of Python," capable of adding more impact to interactive Python sessions by offering high-level data manipulation and visualization commands and courses for the user. An interactive Python session with SciPy becomes an environment that rivals data processing and system prototyping technologies, including "MATLAB, IDL, Octave, R-Lab, and SciLab."

Another advantage of developing "SciPy" on Python, is the accessibility of a strong programming language in the development of advanced programs and specific apps. Scientific apps using SciPy benefit from developers around the globe, developing extra modules in countless software landscape niches. Everything produced has been made accessible to the Python programmer, from database subroutines and classes as well as "parallel programming to web."

These powerful tools are provided along with the "SciPy" mathematical libraries.

IPython (Enhanced Interactive Console)

"IPython (Interactive Python)" is an interface or command shell for interactive computing using a variety of programming languages. "IPython" was initially created exclusively for Python, which supports introspection, rich media, shell syntax, tab completion, and history. Some of the functionalities provided by IPython include: "interactive shells (terminal and Qt-based); browser-based notebook interface with code, text, math, inline plots and other media support; support for interactive data visualization and use of GUI tool kits; flexible interpreters that can be embedded to load into your own projects; tools for parallel computing."

SymPy (Symbolic Mathematics)

Developed by Ondřej Čertík and Aaron Meurer, SymPy is "an open source Python library for symbolic computation." It offers algebra computing abilities to other apps, as a stand-alone app and/or as a library as well as live on the internet applications with "SymPy Live" or "SymPy Gamma." "SymPy" is easy to install and test, owing to the fact that it is completely developed in Python boasting limited dependencies. SymPy involves characteristics ranging from calculus, algebra, discrete mathematics, and quantum physics to fundamental symbolic arithmetic. The outcome of the computations can be formatted as "LaTeX" code. In combination with a straightforward, expandable code base in a widespread programming language, the ease of access provided by SymPy makes it a computer algebra system with a comparatively low entry barrier.

Pandas (Data Structures and Analysis)

Pandas provide highly intuitive and user-friendly high-level data structures. Pandas has achieved popularity in the machine learning algorithm developer community, with built-in techniques for data aggregation, grouping, and filtering as well as results of time series analysis. The Pandas library has two primary structures: one-dimensional "Series" and two-dimensional "Data Frames."

Seaborn (Data Visualization)

Seaborn is derived from the Matplotlib Library and an extremely popular visualization library. It is a high-level library that can generate specific kinds of graph including heat maps, time series, and violin plots.

Installing Scikit-Learn

The latest version of Scikit-Learn can be found on "Scikit-Learn.org" and requires "Python (version >= 3.5); NumPy (version >= 1.11.0); SciPy (version >= 0.17.0); joblib (version >= 0.11)". The plotting capabilities or functions of Scikit-learn start with "plot_" and require "Matplotlib (version >= 1.5.1)". Certain Scikit-Learn examples may need additional applications: "Scikit-Image (version >= 0.12.3), Pandas (version >= 0.18.0)".

With prior installation of "NumPy" and "SciPy," the best method of installing Scikit-Learn is using "pip: pip install -U scikit-learn" or "conda: conda install scikit-learn."

One must make sure that "binary wheels" are utilized when using pip and that "NumPy" and "SciPy" have not been recompiled from source, which may occur with the use of specific OS and hardware settings (for example, "Linux on a Raspberry Pi"). Developing "NumPy" and "SciPy" from source tends to be complicated (particularly on Windows). Therefore, they need to be setup carefully, making sure the optimized execution of linear algebra routines is achievable.

Application of Machine Learning Using Scikit-Learn Library

To understand how Scikit-Learn library is used in the development of a machine learning algorithm, let us use the "Sales_Win_Loss data set from IBM's Watson repository" containing data obtained from sales campaign of a wholesale supplier of automotive parts. We will build a machine learning model to predict which sales campaign will be a winner and which will incur a loss.

The data set can be imported using Pandas and explored using Pandas techniques such as "head (), tail (), and dtypes ()". The plotting techniques from "Seaborn" will be used to visualize the data. To process the data Scikit-Learn's "preprocessing.LabelEncoder ()" will be used and "train_test_split ()" to divide the data set into training subset and testing subset.

To generate predictions from our data set, three different algorithms will be used namely, "Linear Support Vector Classification and K-nearest neighbors classifier". To compare the performances of these algorithms Scikit-Learn library technique "accuracy_score" will be used. The performance score of the models can be visualized using Scikit-Learn and "Yellowbrick" visualization.

Importing the data set

To import the "Sales_Win_Loss data set from IBM's Watson repository", first step is importing the "Pandas" module using *"import pandas as pd"*.

Then we leverage a variable url as
"https://community.watsonanalytics.com/wp content/uploads/2015/04/ WA_Fn-UseC_-Sales-Win-Loss.csv" to store the URL from which the data set will be downloaded.

Now, *"read_csv() as sales_data = pd.read_csv(url)"* technique will be used to read the above "csv or comma separated values" file, which is supplied by the Pandas module. The csv file will then be converted into a Pandas data framework, with the return variable as *"sales_data"*, where the framework will be stored.

For new 'Pandas' users, the *"pd.read csv()"* technique in the code mentioned above will generate a tabular data structure called "data framework", where an index for each row is contained in the first column, and the label / name for each column in the first row are the initial column names acquired from the data set. In the above code snippet, the *"sales data"* variable results in a table depicted in the picture below.

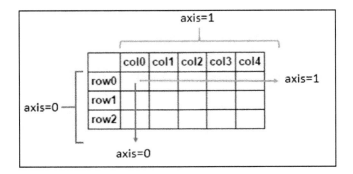

In the diagram above, the "row0, row1, row2" represent individual record index, and the "col0, col1, col2" represent the names for individual columns or features of the data set.

With this step, you have successfully stored a copy of the data set and transformed it into a "Pandas" framework!

Now, using the *"head() as Sales_data.head()"* technique, the records from the data framework can be displayed as shown below to get a "feel" of the information contained in the data set.

	opportunity number	supplies subgroup	supplies group	region	route to market	elapsed days in sales stage	opportunity result
0	1641984	Exterior Accessories	Car Accessories	Northwest	Fields Sales	76	Won
1	1658010	Exterior Accessories	Car Accessories	Pacific	Reseller	63	Loss
2	1674737	Motorcycle Parts	Performance & Non-auto	Pacific	Reseller	24	Won
3	1675224	Shelters & RV	Performance & Non-auto	Midwest	Reseller	16	Loss

Data Exploration

Now that we have our own copy of the data set, which has been transformed it into a "Pandas" data frame, we can quickly explore the data to understand what information can tell can be gathered from it and accordingly to plan a course of action.

In any ML project, data exploration tends to be a very critical phase. Even a fast data set exploration can offer us significant information that could be easily missed otherwise, and this information can propose significant questions that we can then attempt to answer using our project.

Some third-party Python libraries will be used here to assist us with the processing of the data so that we can efficiently use this data with the powerful algorithms of Scikit-Learn. The same *"head()"* technique that we used to see the some initial records of the imported data set in the earlier section can be used here. As a matter of fact, *"(head)"* is effectively capable of doing much more than displaying data records and customize the "head()" technique to display only a selected records with commands like *"sales_data.head(n=2)"*. This command will selectively display the first 2 records of the data set. At a quick glance, it's obvious that columns such as "Supplies Group" and "Region" contain string data, while columns such as "Opportunity Result," "Opportunity Number," etc. are comprised of integer values. It can also be seen that there are unique identifiers for each record in the' Opportunity Number' column.

Similarly, to display select records from the bottom of the table, the *"tail() as sales_data.tail()"* can be used.

To view the different data types available in the data set, the Pandas technique *"dtypes() as sales_data.dtypes"* can be used. With this information, the data columns available in the data framework can be listed with their respective data types. We can figure our, for example, that the column "Supplies Subgroup" is an "object" data type and that the column "Client Size By Revenue" is an "integer data type." So, we have an understanding of columns that either contains integer values or string data.

Data Visualization

At this point, we are through with basic data exploration steps, so we will not attempt to build some appealing plots to portray the information visually and discover other concealed narratives from our data set.

Of all the available Python libraries providing data visualization features; "Seaborn" is one of the best available options, so we will be using the same. Make sure that python plots module provided by "Seaborn" has been installed on your system and ready to be used. Now follow the steps below generate desired plot for the data set:

Step 1 - Import the "Seaborn" module with the command *"import seaborn as sns"*.

Step 2 - Import the "Matplotlib" module with command *"import matplotlib.pyplot as plt"*.

Step 3 - To set the "background color" of the plot as white, use command *"sns.set(style="whitegrid", color_codes=True)"*.

Step 4 - To set the "plot size" for all plots, use command *"sns.set(rc={'figure.figsize':(11.7,8.27)})"*.

Step 5 – To generate a "countplot", use command *"sns.countplot('Route To Market', data=sales_data, hue = 'Opportunity Result')"*.

Step 6 – To remove the top and bottom margins, use command *"sns.despine(offset=10, trim=True)"*.

Step 7 – To display the plot, use command *"plotplt.show()"*.

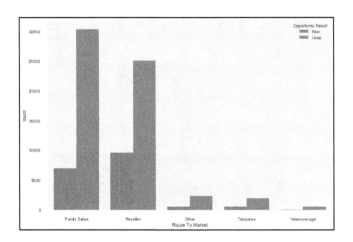

Quick recap - The "Seaborn" and "Matplotlib" modules were imported first. Then the *"set()"* technique was used to define the distinct characteristics for our plot, such as plot style and color. The background of the plot was defined to be white using the code snippet *"sns.set(style= "whitegrid", color codes= True)"*. Then the plot size was define using command *"sns.set(rc={'figure.figsize':(11.7,8.27)})"* that define the size of the plot as "11.7px and 8.27px".

Next the command *"sns.countplot('Route To Market',data= sales data, hue='Opportunity Result')"* was used to generate the plot. The "countplot()" technique enables creation of a count plot, which can expose multiple arguments to customize the count plot according to our requirements. As part of the first *"countplot()"* argument, the X-axis was defined as the column "Route To Market" from the data set. The next argument concerns the source of the data set, which would be "sales_data" data framework we imported earlier. The third argument is the color of the bar graphs that were defined as "blue" for the column labeled "won" and "green" for the column labeled "loss".

Data Pre-processing

By now you should have a clear understanding of what information is available in the data set. From the data exploration step, we established that majority of the columns in our data set are "string data", but "Scikit-Learn" can only process numerical data. Fortunately, the Scikit-Learn library offers us many ways to convert string data into numerical data, for example, *"LabelEncoder()"* technique. To transform categorical labels from the data set such as "won" and "loss" into numerical values, we will use the *"LabelEncoder()"* technique.

Let's look at the pictures below to see what we are attempting to accomplish with the *"LabelEncoder()"* technique. The first image contains one column labeled "color" with three records namely, "Red", "Green" and "Blue". Using the *"LabelEncoder()"* technique, the record in the same "color" column can be converted to numerical values, as shown in the second image.

	Color
0	Red
1	Green
2	Blue

	Color
0	1
1	2
2	3

Let's begin the real process of conversion now. Using the *"fit transform()"* technique given by *"LabelEncoder()"*, the labels in the categorical column like "Route To Market" can be encoded and converted to numerical labels comparable to those shown in the diagrams above. The function *"fit transform()"* requires input labels identified by the user and consequently returns encoded labels.

To know how the encoding is accomplished, let's go through an example quickly. The code instance below constitutes string data in form of a list of cities such as ["Paris", "Paris", "Tokyo", "Amsterdam"] that will be encoded into something comparable to "[2, 2, 1,3]".

Step 1 - To import the required module, use command *"from sklearn import preprocessing"*.

Step 2 – To create the Label encoder object, use command *"le = preprocessing.LabelEncoder()"*.

Step 3 – To convert the categorical columns into numerical values, use command:

```
"encoded_value = le.fit_transform(["Paris",
"Paris", "Tokyo", "Amsterdam"])"

"print(encoded_value) [1 1 2 0]"
```

And there you have it! We just converted our string data labels into numerical values. The first step was importing the preprocessing module that offers the *"LabelEncoder()"* technique. Followed by the development of an object representing the *"LabelEncoder()"* type. Then the *"fit_transform()"* function of the object was used to distinguish between distinct classes of the list ["Paris", "Paris", "Tokyo", "Amsterdam"] and output the encoded values of *"[1 1 2 0]"*.

Did you observe that the *"LabelEncoder()"* technique assigned the numerical values to the classes in alphabetical order according to the initial letter of the classes, for example "(A)msterdam" was assigned code "0", "(P)aris" was assigned code "1" and "(T)okyo" was assigned code "2".

Creating Training and Test subsets

To know the interactions between distinct characteristics and how these characteristics influence the target variable, a ML algorithm must be trained on a collection of information. We need to split the complete data set into two subsets to accomplish this. One subset will serve as the training data set, which will be used to train our algorithm to construct machine learning models. The other subset will serve as the test data set, which will be used to test the accuracy of the predictions generate by the machine learning model.

The first phase in this stage is the separation of feature and target variables using the steps below:

Step 1 – To select data excluding select columns, use command *"select columns other than 'Opportunity Number', 'Opportunity Result' cols = [col for col in sales_data.columns if col not in ['Opportunity Number','Opportunity Result']]"*.

Step 2 – To drop these select columns, use command *"dropping the 'Opportunity Number' and 'Opportunity Result' columns*

data = sales_data[cols]".

Step 3 – To assign the Opportunity Result column as "target", use command *"target = sales_data['Opportunity Result']*

data.head(n=2)".

The "Opportunity Number" column was removed since it just acts as a unique identifier for each record. The "Opportunity Result" contains the predictions we want to generate, so it becomes our "target" variable and can be removed from the data set for this phase. The first line of the above code will select all the columns except "Opportunity Number" and "Opportunity Result" in and assign these columns to a variable "cols." Then using the columns in the "cols" variable, a new data framework was developed. This is going to be the "feature set." Next, the column "Opportunity Result" from the *"sales_data"* data frame was used to develop a new data framework called "target."

The second phase in this stage is to separate the date frameworks into trainings and testing subsets using the steps below. Depending on the data set and desired predictions, it needs to be split into training and testing subset accordingly. For this exercise, we will use 75% of the data as training subset, and rest 25% will be used for the testing subset. We will leverage the *"train_test_split()"* technique in "Scikit-Learn" to separate the data using steps and code as below:

Step 1 – To import required module, use command *"from sklearn.model_selection import train_test_split"*.

Step 2 – To separate the data set, use command *"split data set into train and test setsdata_train, data_test, target_train, target_test = train_test_split(data, target, test_size = 0.30, random_state = 10)"*.

With the code above, the *"train_test_split"* module was first imported, followed by the use of *"train_test_split()"* technique to generate "training subset *(data_train, target_train)*" and "testing subset *(data_test, data_train)*". The *"train_test_split()"* technique's first argument pertains to the features that were divided in the preceding stage; the next argument relates to the target ("Opportunity Result"). The third "test size" argument is the proportion of the data we wish to divide and use as testing subset. We are using 30% for this example, although it can be any amount. The fourth 'random state' argument is used to make sure that the results can be reproduced every time.

Building the Machine Learning Model

The "machine_learning_map" provided by Scikit-Learn is widely used to choose the most appropriate ML algorithm for the data set. For this exercise, we will be using "Linear Support Vector Classification" and "K-nearest neighbors classifier" algorithms.

Linear Support Vector Classification

"Linear Support Vector Classification" or "Linear SVC" is a sub-classification of "Support Vector Machine (SVM)" algorithm, which we have reviewed in chapter 2 of this book titled "Machine Learning Algorithms." Using Linear SVC, the data can be divided into different planes so the algorithm can identify the optimal group structure for all the data classes.

Here are the steps and code for this algorithm to build our first ML model:

Step 1 – To import the required modules, use commands *"from sklearn.svm import LinearSVC"* and *"from sklearn.metrics import accuracy_score"*.

Step 2 – To develop an LinearSVC object type, use command *"svc_model = LinearSVC(random_state=0)"*.

Step 3 – To train the algorithm and generate predictions from the testing data, use command *"pred = svc_model.fit(data_train, target_train).predict(data_test)"*.

Step 4 – To display the model accuracy score, use command *"print ('LinearSVC accuracy:', accuracy_score(target_test, pred, normalize = True))"*.

With the code above, the required modules were imported in the first step. We then developed a type of Linear SVC using *"svc_model"* object with "random_state" as '0'. The "random_state" command instructs the built-in random number generator to shuffle the data in a particular order. In step 3, the "Linear SVC" algorithm is trained on the training data set and subsequently used to generate predictions for the target from the testing data. The *"accuracy_score()"* technique was used in the end to verify the "accuracy score" of the model, which could be displayed as "LinearSVC accuracy : 0.777811004785", for instance.

K-nearest Neighbors Classifier

The "k-nearest neighbors(k-NN)" algorithm is referred to as "a non-parametric method used for classification and regression in pattern recognition". In cases of classification and regression, "the input consists of the nearest k closest training examples in the feature space". K-NN is a form of "instance-based learning", or "lazy learning", in which the function is only locally estimated, and all calculations are delayed until classification. The output is driven by the fact, whether the classification or regression method is used for k-NN:

- "k-nearest neighbors classification" - The "output" is a member of the class. An "object" is classified by its neighbors' plurality vote, assigning the object to the most prevalent class among its nearest "k-neighbors," where "k" denotes a small positive integer. If k= 1, the "object" is simply allocated to the closest neighbor's class.

- "k-nearest neighbors regression" - The output is the object's property value, which is computed as an average of the k-nearest neighbors values.

A helpful method for both classification and regression can be assigning weights to the neighbors' contributions, to allow closer neighbors to make more contributions in the average, compared to the neighbors located far apart. For instance, a known "weighting scheme" is to assign each neighbor a weight of "*1/d*", where "d" denotes the distance from the neighbor. The neighbors are selected from a set of objects for which the "class" (for "k-NN classification") or the feature value of the "object" (for "k-NN regression") is known.

Here are the steps and code for this algorithm to build our next ML model:

Step 1 – To import required modules, use the command *"from sklearn.neighbors import KNeighborsClassifier"* and *"from sklearn.metrics import accuracy_score"*.

Step 2 – To create object of the classifier, use command *"neigh = KNeighborsClassifier(n_neighbors=3)"*.

Step 3 – To train the algorithm, use command *"neigh.fit(data_train, target_train)"*.

Step 4 – To generate predictions, use command *"pred = neigh.predict(data_test)"*.

Step 5 – To evaluate accuracy, use command *"print ('KNeighbors accuracy score:', accuracy_score(target_test, pred))"*.

With the code above, the required modules were imported in the first step. We then developed the object *"neigh"* of type "KNeighborsClassifier" with the volume of neighbors as *"n_neighbors=3"*. In the next step, the *"fit()"* technique was used to train the algorithm on the training data set. Next, the model was tested on the testing data set using *"predict()"* technique. Finally, the accuracy score was obtained, which could be *"KNeighbors accuracy score : 0.814550580998"*, for instance.

Now that our preferred algorithms have been introduced, the model with the highest accuracy score can be easily selected. But wouldn't it be great if we had a way to compare the distinct models' efficiency visually? In Scikit-Learn, we can use the "Yellowbrick library", which offers techniques for depicting various scoring techniques visually.

Conclusion

Thank you for making it through to the end of *Python for Data Science: Python Programming Guide to Master Big Data Analysis, Machine Learning, and Artificial Intelligence* let's hope it was informative and able to provide you with all of the tools you need to achieve your goals whatever they may be.

The next step is to make the best use of your new-found wisdom of Python programming, data science, data analysis, and machine learning that have resulted in the birth of the powerhouse, which is the "Silicon Valley." Businesses across the industrial spectrum with an eye on the future are gradually turning into big technology companies under the shadow of their intended business model. This has been proven with the rise of the "FinTech" industry attributed to the financial institutions and enterprises across the world. This book is filled with real-life examples to help you understand the nitty-gritty of the underlying concepts along with the names and descriptions of multiple tools that you can further explore and selectively implement to make sound choices for the development of a desired machine learning model. Now that you have finished reading this book and mastered the use of Python programming, you are all set to start developing your own Python based machine learning model as well as performing big data analysis using all the open sources readily available and explicitly described in this book. With an understanding of how much is at stake for your business and how you can position yourself to not only retain existing customers but also interest more prospective customers that will eventually be converted to a paying consumer, you are poised to take your business to new heights. Start with one step at a time and understand the current status and challenges of your business, then mindfully use the power of data science technologies like artificial intelligence, machine learning, data mining and big data analytics, in your company to be able to enhance human abilities without undermining the human intelligence and creating new high paying and rewarding jobs.

Finally, if you found this book useful in any way, a review on Amazon is always appreciated!

I want to share with you a free sneak peek to another one of my book that I think you will enjoy. The book is called "Python for Beginners Master Data Science, Artificial Intelligence and Machine Learning with this Smart Python Programming Language Guide"

Are you new to software development and looking for a breakthrough in the world of machine learning and artificial intelligence?

Then you have found just the book you need to understand master the **Python programming language** to develop a winning **machine learning model** as well as gain a solid understanding of the fundamentals of data science, machine learning, and artificial intelligence technology.

Python programming language has rendered itself as the language of choice for coding beginners and advanced software programmers alike. This book is written to help you master the basic concepts of Python coding and how you can utilize your coding skills to analyze a large volume of data and uncover valuable information that can otherwise be easily lost in the volume.

Python was designed primarily to emphasize the readability of the programming code, and its syntax enables programmers to convey ideas using fewer lines of code.

Python programming language increases the speed of operation while allowing for higher efficiency in creating system integrations.

Python for Beginners

Master Data Science, Artificial Intelligence and

Machine Learning with this Smart Python

Programming Language Guide

Introduction

Congratulations on purchasing **Python For Beginners:** *Master Data Science, Artificial Intelligence and Machine Learning with this Smart Python Programming Language Guide,* and thank you for doing so.

The following chapters will discuss the core concepts of Data Science, Artificial Intelligence and Machine Learning in the light of Python programming language to provide you a holistic understanding of all the latest cutting-edge technologies. In the first chapter, you will learn the basics of the data science technology with an in-depth overview of the most widely used data science lifecycle called Team Data Science Process (TDSP). You will also learn how Machine learning allows analysis of large volumes of data and delivers faster and more accurate results. There are four different machine learning algorithms described in this book that can be used to cater to the desired data set for the creation of a successful machine learning model. The modern-day high-tech businesses are digging through their past with an eye on the future and this is where artificial intelligence for marketing takes center stage with groundbreaking usage of predictive analytics technology. This chapter will provide you explicit details on how businesses are able to apply a predictive analytics model to gain an understanding of how their customers are interacting with their products and services, as driven by their feelings or emotions shared on the social media platforms.

Chapter 2 will provide a detailed overview of Python and its historical development. Step by step instructions to install Python on your operating systems have also been included. The concept of Python comments, variables and data types that serve as a prerequisite to the learning of Python programming have been explained in detail. It also includes a detailed overview of the basic concepts of Python programming focusing on various programming elements such as Booleans, Tuples, Sets, Dictionaries and much more. The nuances of how to write efficient and effective Python codes have been explained in detail along with plenty of examples and sample exercises to help you solidify your understanding of these concepts.

Chapter 3 pertains to the advanced Python programming concepts that are relatively more complicated and require a solid understanding of the basic concepts. You will learn how to use object-oriented programing concepts, different loops, and conditional statements to write sophisticated commands. Each concept is explained with standard syntax, relevant sample code and practice exercises. It also contains a detailed overview of Django which is a Python-based web framework that is popularly used in the development of web-based programs and applications. You will learn how to install Django on your computer and follow the step by step Python coding instructions to develop your own web-based program and notes taking application.

There are plenty of books on this subject on the market, thanks again for choosing this one! Every effort was made to ensure it is full of as much useful information as possible; please enjoy!

CHAPTER 1

Intro to Data Science Technologies

In the world of technology, Data is defined as "information that is processed and stored by a computer." Our continuous online presence has flooded our realities with data. From a click on a website to the ability of our smartphones to track and record our location throughout the day, our existential world is drowning in the data. We could potentially extract solutions to even those problems that we have not encountered yet from the depth of this humongous data. This very process of gathering insights from a measurable set of data using mathematical equations and statistics can be defined as "data science." The role of data scientists tends to be very versatile and can easily be confused with that of a statistician and a computer scientist. Essentially anyone, be it an individual or a company, that is willing to dig deep through large volume of data to gather information can be referred to as a data science practitioner. For example, companies like Macy's and Nordstrom keep a track on and record of all in-store and online purchases made by the customers, to provide personalized recommendations on products and services. The social media platforms like Facebook that allow the users to list their current location are equipped to identify global migration patterns by analyzing this treasure trove of data that is practically handed over to the company by the users themselves.

The earliest recorded use of the term data science goes back to 1960 and credited to "Peter Naur," who reportedly used the term data science as a substitute for computer science and eventually introduced the term "datalogy." In 1974, Naur published a book titled "Concise Survey of Computer Methods," with liberal use of the term data science throughout the book. In 1992, the contemporary definition of data science was proposed at "The Second Japanese-French Statistics Symposium," with the acknowledgment of emergence of a new discipline focused primarily on types, dimensions and structures of data.

"Data science continues to evolve as one of the most promising and in-demand career paths for skilled professionals. Today, successful data professionals understand that they must advance past the traditional skills of analyzing large amounts of data, data mining, and programming skills. In order to uncover useful intelligence for their organizations, data scientists must master the full

spectrum of the data science life cycle and possess a level of flexibility and understanding to maximize returns at each phase of the process."

– University of California, Berkley

Thanks to the increasing interest of business executives there has been a significant rise in popularity of the term data science. A large section of journalists and academic experts have not acknowledged data science as a separate area of study from the field of statistics. However, a subsection within the same community considers data science is the popular term used for "data mining" and "big data." The very definition of data science is up for debate within the tech community. The field of study that requires a combination of skill set including computer programming skills, domain expertise and proficiency in statistics and mathematical algorithms to be able to extract valuable insight from large volumes of raw data is referred to as data science.

Data Science Lifecycle

The most highly recommended lifecycle to structured data science projects the "Team Data Science Process" (TDSP). This process is widely used for projects that require the deployment of applications based on artificial intelligence and/or machine learning algorithms. It can also be customized for and used in the execution of "exploratory data science" projects as well as "ad hoc analytics" projects. The TDSP lifecycle is designed as an agile and sequential iteration of steps that serve as guidance on the tasks required for the use of predictive models. These predictive models need to be deployed in the production environment of the company, so they can be used in the development of artificial intelligence-based applications. The aim of this data science lifecycle is high-speed delivery and completion of data science projects toward a defined engagement endpoint. Seamless execution of any data science project requires effective communication of tasks within the team as well as to the stakeholders.

The fundamental components of the "Team Data Science Process" are:

Definition of a Data Science Lifecycle

The five major stages of the TDSP lifecycle that outline the interactive steps required for project execution from start to finish are: "Business understanding," "Data acquisition in understanding," "modeling," "deployment" and "customer acceptance." Keep reading for details on this to come shortly!

Standardized Project Structure

To enable seamless and easy access to project documents for the team members allowing for quick retrieval of information, use of templates and a shared directory structure goes a long way. All project documents and the project code our store and a "version control system" such as "TFS," "Git" or "Subversion" for improved team collaboration. Business requirements and associated tasks and functionalities are stored in an agile project tracking system like "JIRA," "Rally," and "Azure DevOps" to enable enhanced tracking of code for every single functionality. These tools also help in the estimation of resources and costs involved through the project lifecycle. To ensure effective management of each project, information security, and team collaboration, TDSP confers in the creation of separate storage for each project on the version control system. The adoption of a standardized structure for all the projects within an organization, aid in creation of an institutional knowledge library across the organization.

The TDSP lifecycle provides standard templates for all the required documents as well as folder structure at a centralized location. The files containing programming codes for the data exploration and extraction of the functionality can be organized to using the provided folder structure, which also holds records pertaining to model iterations. These templates allow the team members to easily understand the work that has been completed by others as well as for a seamless addition of new team members to a given project. The markdown format supports ease of accessibility as well as making edits or updates to the document templates. To make sure the project goal and objectives are well defined and also to ensure the expected quality of the deliverables, these templates provide various checklists with important questions for each project. For example, a "project charter" can be used to document the project scope and the business problem that is being resolved by the project; standardized data reports are used to document the "structure and statistics" of the data.

Infrastructure and Resources for Data Science Projects

To effectively store infrastructure and manage shared analytics, the TDSP recommends using tools like: "machine learning service," databases, "big data clusters," and cloud-based systems to store data sets. The analytics and storage infrastructure that houses raw as well as processed or cleaned data sets can be cloud-based or on-premises. D analytics and storage infrastructure permits the reproducibility of analysis and prevents duplication and the redundancy of data that can create inconsistency and unwarranted infrastructure costs, which no one wants. Tools are supplied to grant specific permissions to the shared resources and to track their activity which in turn allows secure access to the resources for each member of the team.

Tools and Utilities for Project Execution

The introduction of any changes to an existing process tends to be rather challenging in most organizations. To encourage and raise the consistency of adoption of these changes several tools can be implemented that are provided by the TDSP. Some of the basic tasks in the data science lifecycle, including "data exploration" and "baseline modeling," can be easily automated with the tools provided by TDSP. To allow the hassle-free contribution of shared tools and utilities into the team's "shared code repository," TDSP from provides a well-defined structure. This results in cost savings by allowing other project teams within the organization to reuse and repurpose these shared tools and utilities.

The TDSP lifecycle serves as a standardized template with a well-defined set of artifacts that can be used to garner effective team collaboration and communication across the board. This lifecycle is comprised of a selection of the best practices and structures from "Microsoft" to facilitated successful delivery predictive analytics Solutions and intelligent applications.

Artificial Intelligence

Human beings or Homo Sapiens, often tout themselves as being the most superior species to have ever housed the planet Earth, ascribing primarily to their "intelligence." Even the most complex animal behavior is never considered as intelligent; however, the simplest of human behavior is ascribed to intelligence. For example, when a female digger wasp returns with food to her burrow, she deposits the food on the threshold and checks for intruders prior to carrying her food inside. Sounds like an intelligent wasp, right? But an experiment conducted on these wasps, where the scientist displaced the food not too far from the entrance of the burrow while the wasp was inside, revealed that the wasps continued to reiterate the whole procedure every time the food was moved from its original location. This experiment concluded that inability of the wasp to adapt to the changing circumstances and thereby "intelligence," is noticeably absent in the wasps. So what is this "human intelligence"? Psychologists characterize human intelligence as a composite of multiple abilities such as learning from experiences and being able to adapt accordingly, understanding abstract concepts, reasoning, problem-solving, use of language and perception.

The science of developing human-controlled and operated machinery, such as digital computers or robots that can mimic human intelligence adapt to new inputs and perform human-like tasks are called "Artificial Intelligence" (AI). Thanks to Hollywood, most people think of robots coming to life and wreaking havoc on the planet, when they hear the words Artificial Intelligence. But that is far from the truth. The core principle of Artificial Intelligence is the ability of the AI-powered machines to rationalize (think like humans) and take actions (mimic human actions) towards fulfilling the targeted goal. Simply put, Artificial Intelligence is the creation of a machine that will think and act like humans. The three paramount goals of Artificial Intelligence are learning, reasoning and perception.

Although the term Artificial Intelligence was coined in 1956, the British pioneer of Computer Sciences, Alan Mathison Turing, performed groundbreaking work in the field of Artificial Intelligence, in the mid-20th century. In 1935, Turing developed an abstract computing machine with a scanner and unlimited memory in the form of symbols. The scanner was capable of moving back and forth through the memory, reading the existing symbols as well as writing further symbols of the memory. A programming instruction would dictate the actions of the scanner and was also stored in the memory. Thus, Turing generated a machine with implicit learning capabilities that could modify and improve its own programming. This concept is widely known as the universal "Turing Machine" and serves as a basis for all modern computers. Turing claimed that computers could learn from their own experience and solve problems using a guiding principle known as "heuristic problem-solving."

In the 1950s, the early AI research was primarily focused on problem-solving and symbolic methods. By the 1960s, the AI research had a major leap of interest from "The US Department of Defense," who started working towards training computers to mirror human reasoning. In the 1970s, the "Defense Advanced Research

Projects Agency" (DARPA) has successfully completed its street mapping projects. It might come to you as a surprise, that DARPA actually produced intelligent personal assistants in 2003, long before the existence of the famous Siri and Alexa. Needless to say, this groundbreaking work in the field of AI has paved the way for automation and reasoning observed in the modern-day computers.

Here are the core human traits that we aspire to mimic in the machines:

1. **Knowledge** – In order for machines to be able to act and react like humans, they require an abundance of data and information pertaining to the world around us. To be able to implement knowledge engineering AI must have seamless access to data objects, data categories, and data properties as well as the relationship between them that can be managed and stored in the separate data storages.

2. **Learning** – Of all the different forms of learning applicable to AI, the simplest one is the "trial and error" method. For example, a chess learning computer program will try all possible moves until the mate-in-one move is found to end the game. This move is then stored by the program to be used the next time it encounters the same position. This relatively easy to implement an aspect of learning called "rote learning," involves simple memorization of individual items and procedures. The most challenging part of the learning is

called "generalization," which involves applying the past experience to the corresponding new scenarios.

3. **Problem-solving** – The systematic process to reach a predefined goal or solution by searching through a range of possible actions can be defined as problem-solving. The problem-solving techniques can be customized for a particular problem or used for a wide variety of problems. A general-purpose problem-solving method frequently used in AI is "means-end analysis," which involves a step-by-step deduction of the difference between the current state and final state of the goal. Think about some of the basic functions of a robot, such as back and forth movements or picking up stuff, that lead to fulfillment of a goal.

4. **Reasoning** – The act of reasoning can be defined as the ability to draw inferences that are appropriate to the given situation. The two forms of reasoning are called "deductive reasoning" and "inductive reasoning." In deductive reasoning, if the premise is true then the conclusion is assumed to be true. On the other hand, the inductive reasoning, even if the premise is true, the conclusion may or may not be true. Although considerable success has been achieved in programming computers to perform deductive reasoning, the implementation of "true reasoning" remains aloof and one of the biggest challenges facing Artificial Intelligence.

5. **Perception** – The process of generating a multidimensional view of an object by means of various sensory organs can be defined as perception. This creation of awareness of the environment is complicated by a number of factors, such as the viewing angle, the direction and intensity of the light and the amount of contrast produced by the object, with the surrounding field. Breakthrough developments have been made in the field of artificial perception and can be easily observed in our daily life with the advent of self-driving cars and robots that can collect empty soda cans while moving through the buildings.

If you enjoyed this preview of my book "Python for Beginners", be sure to check out the full book on Amazon or the audiobook on Audible (free copy with the link above).

Some of the highlights of the book include:

- Key features and advantages of learning to code Python as well as the history of how Python programming was created.

- Step by step instructions on how to install Python on your operating systems (Windows, Mac, and Linux).

- The concept of Python data types is presented in exquisite detail with various examples of each data type.

- Learn how to create Python variables and assign desired data type to them.

- Basic concepts of writing efficient and effective Python codes, focusing on various programming elements such as Booleans, Tuples, Sets, Dictionaries, and much more.

- Learn how to write if and else statements to retrieve desired information from your data.

- For and While loops are explained with explicit details in an easy to understand language.

- Learn the advanced coding concepts of Python Functions, Modules, Inheritance as well as File and Exception Handling.

- And much, much more...

All the concepts are explained with standard Python coding syntax supported with relevant **examples** and followed by **exercises** to help you test and verify your understanding of those concepts.

Finally, as an added bonus, you will learn some **Python tips and tricks** to take your machine learning programming game to the next level.

Remember, knowledge is power, and with the great power you will gather from this book, you will be armed to make sound personal and professional technological choices. Your Python programming skillset will improve drastically, and you will be poised to develop your very own machine learning model!

Even if you don't have any knowledge of Python, but still want to become more experienced in this field as soon as possible, then the best thing you can do is buy this book now!